A Day in the Life of
British Rail

A Day in the Life of British Rail

Edited by

Murray Brown

Editor of **RAIL**

DAVID & CHARLES
Newton Abbot   London

British Library Cataloguing in Publication Data

A day in the life of British Rail.
  1. Great Britain. Railway services. British rail
  I. Brown, Murray *1947–*
  385′.0941

   ISBN 0-7153-9324-3

© EMAP National Publications Ltd 1989

Typeset by Typesetters (Birmingham) Ltd
Smethwick, West Midlands
and printed in West Germany
by Mohdruck GmbH
for David & Charles Publishers plc
Brunel House Newton Abbot Devon

CONTENTS

INTRODUCTION

Taking one day out of BR's continuous activity is a fascinating exercise. The organisation which the public loves and hates is a multi-million pound business whose activities extend far beyond a mere twenty-four hours. With 154,700 staff of which 133,500 are directly concerned with the actual railway, BR has an amazing multitude of vocations ranging from railman to the BRB Chairman, from solicitors to Director of Industrial Design.

From Wick and Thurso to Penzance, BR has 10,335 route miles of which 8,887 miles are used by passenger trains. On this network are 2,425 stations and there are 1,426 miles electrified with 25kV overhead and 1,188 miles electrified with a third rail.

Traction and rolling stock numbers are also impressive. There are some 2,040 diesels of which 518 are shunting locomotives; 230 electric locomotives are on the books and BR has 2,382 diesel multiple units with a further 7,022 units of electric traction. You can ride in 2,891 coaches (including 192 sleepers) or in 712 High Speed Train trailer cars powered by 197 power cars.

Although BR is one of the last bastions of a nationalised industry, privatisation has already, quietly and unnoticed, made significant inroads in the last two decades. Catering, some engineering works and a sizeable proportion of freight rolling stock is now in private hands, the latter, for instance, equating to some 14,000 vehicles.

A typical (if that can be defined) summer Friday was selected as 'The Day' and this album endeavours to portray some of the varied activities and people which (and who) make up this great industry. Many events and actions do not occur daily and accordingly it would have been easy to include examples which did not happen on the day in question. Two such events include a train smash and the Royal train in action, the former unfortunately and the latter fortunately. There are many more examples but, nevertheless, every day sees a wealth of human and train activity and many are illustrated in this book.

The spectacular backdrop of the Forth Bridge is the setting for this daily freight service which runs from Thornton to Edinburgh Millerhill Yard each day. A class 26 locomotive is providing the power as the train enters Dalmeny. (*Photo Douglas Young*)

(*Overleaf*) The 35-strong fleet of class 87 locomotives are used on West Coast main line duties. One of them, No 87026 *Sir Richard Arkwright* powers the 08.35 Euston–Inverness The Clansman service past Beck Foot south of Carlisle. (*Photo Peter J. Robinson*)

To the ordinary man or woman in the street, the operation of British Rail will mean little more than the actual running of trains, be they passenger or freight. However, the running of the 08.00 King's Cross to Edinburgh High Speed Train over the East Coast main line requires an army of workers ranging from the railman at King's Cross to the InterCity Manager at York and even perhaps, the InterCity Director, himself, if an embracing policy decision has to be made. The mention of York is perhaps opportune to reflect the variety of railway vocations which exist at this major railway centre. York is steeped in railway history and yet it is in the forefront of the modern railway, as the £306m electrification scheme for the East Coast main line takes in the capital of Yorkshire.

Besides the railmen, station inspectors and announcer (who sits in the signalbox near platform 13) there are many other operational staff whose identities are not recognisable, but whose presence is vital. Carriage and wagon staff and engineering fitters are always on hand to cater for unexpected occurrences, such as a broken window on an HST, or to give attention to a power car or locomotive which is losing its coolant and is therefore likely to shut down. Have you ever thought about who maintains the lift or the lights, the signals or the points, or the telephones? The left luggage office sees much business, as does the inquiry bureau and the booking office. The Post Office staff are always within sight as York is served by several Travelling Post Office trains. And why is there a red carpet in the Area Manager's storeroom? York is frequently visited by royalty and the visits of such dignitaries require weeks of planning and arrangements – on top of running the daily train service.

Because York station retains so much of its character, it has been the venue for numerous film location-shoots, including *Race to the North*

There's a splash of colour in Yorkshire these days – the class 141 twin unit railbuses are receiving the much admired livery of the West Yorkshire Passenger Transport Authority as the units are modified at Andrew Barclay's Works at Kilmarnock. This unit was sitting in the bay at York station waiting for its next duty to Selby. (*Photo R. Ashby*)

One of the dedicated class 37 locomotives based at Laira depot, Plymouth, for working the Cornish china clay traffic winds its way down the picturesque branch to Fowey Docks at Golant with a load of china clay for export. The 125 wagons used for this traffic are owned by BR, although they carry the markings of English China Clay (ECC). (*Photo Stephen McGahon*)

and *Agatha* where Dustin Hoffman strolled down platform 8! For these filming requirements, arrangements are dealt with by the staff from the public relations office at the nearby regional headquarters building in York. Staff have the unenviable duty of ensuring that the film-makers obtain their period sequences without the intrusion of a modern day railway and yet allow the modern day railway to function normally.

A railway never stays the same and the 25kV overhead wires have now been strung up at York in preparation for the power to be switched on and electric trains run. Before this can happen, all the signals have to be immunised against the effects of the electric current and the staff trained in the vagaries of electric-powered trains. Not only that, but because York station is a Grade I listed building, the Fine Arts Commission and the York City Fathers have to be consulted as to the visual effects of the overhead wires. This applies to other structures along the East Coast main line, such as the viaducts and bridges at Durham, Morpeth, and the Royal Border Bridge at Berwick.

York is also the centre for the north east office of the Transport Users Consultative Committee, the public watchdog which looks after the interests of rail-users. This office sees the forthcoming timetable and comments thereon if the TUCC feels that the public's interest could be better served. A BR liaison manager is nominated in the headquarters building offices to which the matters for discussion are presented. The TUCC is also involved when BR wishes to close a line to passenger use. The TUCC has the power to arrange a public hearing where objectors to the closure can air their views.

At every railway centre can be seen the yellow track machines which tend to every feature of the permanent way. York is no exception and in the Leeman Road sidings can be seen a variety of these highly complex and expensive machines which can lift track, tamp it (consolidate the ballast), level it and even stabilise it so that trains can actually run at full

The Sprinter revolution has come to the Cambrian Lines, although the new units do not offer passengers a forward view through the driver's windows. Pensarn is the location of this picture as a Machynlleth-Pwllheli service passes by. These Sprinter units are based at Derby Etches Park depot for maintenance purposes. (*Photo J. Tickner*)

(*Overleaf*) The class 86 fleet of locomotives are used on the West Coast main line and also on services between Liverpool Street and Cambridge. Pictured at Greenholme at the head of the 14.30 Euston–Glasgow is 86220, *The Round Tabler*. (*Photo Peter J. Robinson*)

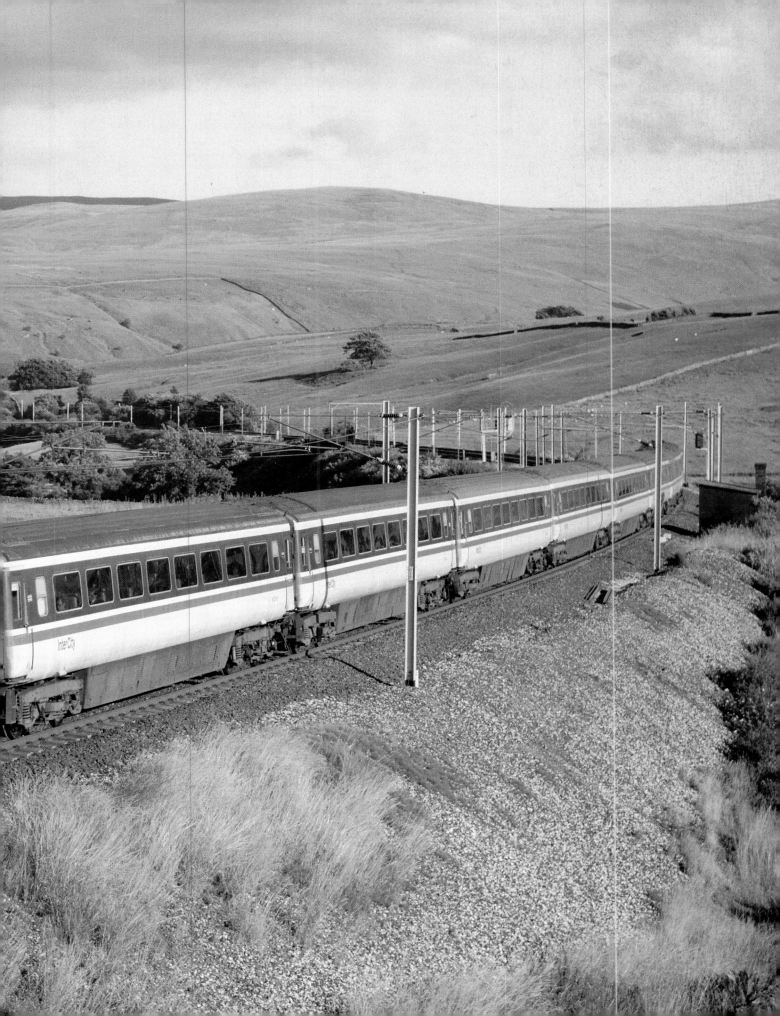

speed over renewed track immediately after the work has been completed. These track machines are built in Austria by Plasser & Theurer who supply their machines worldwide, and others are by Matisa and built in Switzerland.

Whilst York is a regional centre, Derby is the technical centre of BR and the Railway Technical Centre buildings at Derby house another vast number of activities, many of which the public have no idea exist, but which are all so vital to the running of the railway. In Trent House can be found many of the engineering departments associated with the businesses of the railway. The engineers who investigate problems and plan new technology for both locomotives and rolling stock also deal with private firms who wish to run their vehicles on BR tracks. Inspecting engineers not only have to check new items of stock for safety and make sure that they comply with health and safety standards, but they also inspect venerable steam locomotives to ascertain whether they comply with the safety criteria laid down for the operation of steam traction on BR tracks.

All good things come to an end and the offices which deal with the disposal of all condemned stock can be found in Trent House and Derwent House. The Central Repair & Contract Centre is the clearing office for all repairs and condemnations, and if a vehicle is withdrawn from service, it is then offered to the Director of Procurement who makes

'We can't go on meeting like this' . . . old and new diesel multiple units come face to face at Cambridge after a day's work during which time they will have covered over 1,000 miles' duty. On the left is a vintage 30-year-old Metro-Cammell-built unit confronting the latest DMU technology – a brand new class 156 Sprinter multiple unit, also a product of Metro-Cammell, Birmingham. The new unit is part of a fleet which works the East Anglia–Birmingham or North West services (Liverpool or Blackpool) whilst the old unit is used for domestic services within East Anglia. (*Photo Gordon Bird*)

In darkest Cambridgeshire – a rural by-water near Ely to be precise – is the setting for a familiar occurrence. This Dutch tourist must feel quite at home with the flat lands of East Anglia, a mirror image of his native land. Driving on the left and the quaint crossing gates, however, must be an anathema! One of BR's second series of new Sprinter trains, a class 150/2, hurries past, a vast improvement on the standard of comfort endured by East Anglian rail travellers on the veteran Cravens-built multiple units (now extinct) and the surviving Metro-Cammel units which still traverse these Provincial sector lines. (*Photo Gordon Bird*)

Shortages of Pacer multiple units in the North-West was a major problem for BR in the summer of 1988 and locomotive hauled coaches were regularly substituted. Here, a class 31 locomotive powers a Manchester Victoria-Blackburn train, which is seen approaching the closed station of Sough. (*Photo M. A. Kirby*)

the details known to prospective purchasers in a tender document. Many coaches and wagons end their days in a breaker's yard and the paperwork and arrangements are all controlled from Derby. BR's central record office is situated here, known as the Rolling Stock Library – a fascinating database of thousands of records which would keep a railway historian in a permanent state of euphoria!

Kelvin House is the headquarters of BR's Research Department. BR is acknowledged by railway systems worldwide as being in the forefront of railway engineering technology, and this work continues. Not only are vehicles and equipment tested; the Research Department examines many other aspects of railway life including the fire resistance of fabrics and the development of special paints. BR even has two special test tracks not far from Derby where new vehicles are put through their paces under controlled conditions, without the hindrance of a normal service to contend with. These two test tracks are at Old Dalby near Melton Mowbray, and Mickleover to the west of Derby.

There are many depots around the country where traction, rolling stock, plant and machinery and road vehicles – yes, BR has hundreds of road vehicles for use by maintenance staff – are maintained, and some of these depots have their own emergency lifting gear in case of derailments and accidents. All of BR's cranes are now diesel powered, the last steam crane having retired as recently as 1988! Although accidents are few, minor derailments are fairly common and Bruff vehicles are allocated to some depots, being able to run on rails and also roads. They are fitted with hydraulic gear which enables ends of vehicles to be raised and slewed back onto the tracks.

London is the administrative centre for much of BR's activities. Here, in a variety of locations, can be found further activities which help run this great business. For instance, Tournament House in Paddington station houses InterCity On-board Services whose staff plan, organise and implement the catering side of train services. Not all catering, however, is provided by this organisation for, in accordance with government policy, there are now numerous private caterers offering a trolley service, particularly on cross-country trains (the Provincial Services). One such private firm is Right Lines whose staff ply up and down the class 156 Sprinter trains which run between the North West and East Anglia. Also based in Tournament House is InterCity's Charter Train Unit. Want to hire a train to take a party to the Ideal Home Exhibition? Alternatively,

A North East–South West HST hurries over the River Avon at Eckington, Gloucestershire in the late afternoon. The HSTs on this route linking Plymouth/Bristol/Sheffield and on to Leeds or Newcastle can be identified from their sister trains on the East Coast main line as they have seven coaches as opposed to eight. The smaller formation is produced by having only one first class coach instead of two. (*Photo Hugh Ballantyne*)

do you fancy taking a trip in the luxury land cruise The West Highlander? It is all managed from this building.

Meanwhile, across the city at Waterloo, can be found some of the managers who run the Network SouthEast sector, the largest urban railway system in the world. During the peak period, a train arrives at a London terminal every eleven seconds. With the coming of the Channel Tunnel, BR has made provision for a brand new organisation to plan and execute all the activities associated with this multi-million pound construction project. This, too, is based at Waterloo.

Not far from Liverpool Street station is the headquarters of BR's Property Board which manages this organisation's vast property interests. These range from a humble rent for the use of a space beneath a tunnel arch to the liaison with conglomerates who have millions of pounds to develop station sites, which includes the complete rebuilding of stations.

Heading a Speedlink coal train to Westbury is one of Railfreight's class 37 locomotives bearing the 'Red Stripe' livery. The train is seen at Bradford-on-Avon. This livery is now superseded by the new Railfreight colours of triple grey with the business sub-sector symbol. Some will be sorry to see the 'Red Stripe' livery vanish as the use of red greatly enhanced the appearance of locomotives. (*Photo N. K. Welford*)

BR is a large landowner and the sale of surplus land is big business, bringing in millions of pounds every year.

Near Marylebone station is Blandford House and you will not get in here easily! Security is the order of the day at this location, for Blandford House is where some of BR's huge computer machinery is kept, including the real-time Total Operations Processing System (TOPS) which can tell any inquirer the whereabouts of any locomotive, wagon or coach in the country, what its state is, and any information as to its maintenance history.

Much of BR's business is aided by computer technology and there are several centres around the country where large computers provide data and back-up systems, such as for the payroll and pensions of BR staff. Crewe, Nottingham and Darlington are three such computer centres.

The nerve centre of British Rail is at Euston House next to Euston station. The sector directors are based here, together with many of their staff. Also domiciled in this building are the staff who deal with you, the public. Every day, BR receives many inquiries from the media and the BRB Press Office is kept exceptionally busy, particularly if a major press conference is taking place or if there has been a major accident.

Read all about it! *Rail News*, BR's own newspaper, is compiled and edited on the first floor of Euston House where Keith Horrocks has been the editor for twenty years. Every member of staff throughout the country receives a free copy and *Rail News* is available for sale to the general public.

Up on the sixth floor can be found the figurehead of BR, the Chairman, Sir Robert Reid who, because of his outstanding ability, had his term of office extended by the Secretary of State for Transport. Sir Bob presides over his Board, which meets regularly to run what is now one of the last surviving, large state industries.

In these pages, you will read about, and see many photographs depicting the varied duties of railway staff throughout the country. Some jobs are unusual, some are mundane, but all are part and parcel of the running of this nationalised transport system. It is a twenty-four-hour-a-day industry and some parts of BR are more busy at night than by day. It is hoped that the images contained within this book's pages will provide much entertainment and thought as they portray how this much maligned, but nevertheless highly impressive and, nowadays, efficient, railway system functions.

It can be just as busy at night as during the day when it comes to BR operations. Bristol Bath Road depot services locomotives used for parcels work and consequently is a busy nocturnal location. Bristol also has a depot nearby (St Philips Marsh) which maintains some of the HST fleet. Class 31 and 47 locomotives repose under the floodlights ready for another day's work. (*Photo Mike Goodfield*)

They don't leave a stone unturned . . . the permanent way men are another hardened breed of railwaymen whose work entails a sizeable input of calories. They toil through all weathers and whilst their vocation has the use of highly mechanised machines, there is also much manual effort expended on the track, taken for granted by most passengers. Ronnie Scott (left) was the lookout man for Bill Thomas as he carried out maintenance work at Newcastle Central station. (*Photo Robin Trinder*)

Arriving at Euston station from Northampton is a class 317 unit No 317306. This type of unit is new to the Euston–Northampton services, the class 317 units previously working the Bedford–St Pancras services. With the advent of the brand new class 319 'Thameslink' trains on the Bedford–St Pancras/King's Cross–Gatwick line, the class 317s have migrated – some to the aforementioned Euston line and others to the King's Cross–Peterborough/Cambridge routes where business has risen by some 300% in the last four years. (*Photo Dr Iain C. Scotchman*)

Having received an overhaul at Bath Road depot, Bristol, power car No 43191 is moved into Marsh Junction depot where the painters set to work transforming the old InterCity livery into the latest IC colour scheme, incorporating the swallow logo. (*Photo Mike Goodfield*)

At Marsh Junction depot, Bristol, welder Ken Griffiths fabricates a new steps for the civil engineer's track machine. All the Bristol based track machines are serviced at Marsh Junction. (*Photo Mike Goodfield*)

A busy scene at Sevington where the double-headed class 33s are propelling 18 empty hopper wagons en route to Snowdon Colliery whilst in the background a train of 36 limestone hopper wagons from Whatley Quarry is being unloaded. (*Photo I. G. Feather*)

A DAY IN THE LIFE OF BR

The extent to which our railways have changed from common carrier to essentially a passenger concern is never clearer than at night. Gone are the days when, if you lived within a few miles of virtually any main line, you could hear regular, if not continuous, activity during the small hours, when almost wherever you were in city Britain on a clear night the sound of distant clanging of wagons in freight yards and the puffing of shunting engines came wafting in. A lot of trains still run at night, but a much higher proportion are passenger, and even the freight ones – notably Freightliners between England and Scotland – travel at what a generation ago would have been regarded as high passenger speed. Once the signalmen in hundreds of manual boxes along our main lines boasted they were kept as busy by night as day, with perhaps a slight difference that trains were longer in the section. Very few manual boxes are now open around the clock, and multiple aspect signals change from red to yellow, to double yellow and green, with eerie speed as the owl hoots.

As the new day begins at midnight – memories of how the whistles of thousands of locomotives rang out into the night as the railways became the nation's on that 1 January, now over forty years ago – a handful of HSTs (mostly on the East Coast main line) are still completing yesterday's journeys. But the peak activity is in the maintenance depots. From Aberdeen to Penzance the task of keeping the HSTs available for their daily 'flight' has almost more in common with aircraft management than the traditional railway even of early BR days. Nothing has changed more dramatically than stock utilisation. Our typical day saw its own examples of commuter trains cancelled and charter traffic turned away through the lack of availability of stock. But it was the HSTs that in the summer of 1988 were still bearing the brunt of InterCity's business on the East Coast main line, as well as out of Paddington and at St Pancras. Many sets work long diagrams such as Inverness–King's Cross–Leeds. BR can no more afford to have HSTs idle than can BA its 747s.

There is an organised frenzy of activity as the sets roll into the larger depots with reports of the previous day's faults. The forecast of when they will become available for the next day's traffic carries all the excitement of overnight election results. Occasionally a final adjustment may indeed be made by a key man from a depot as the train goes into a terminus such as King's Cross to pick up its first load, a special stop being made to set him back at depot as the set begins its revenue earning. Appearances are always deceptive; the man has not arranged quick transport home!

But most overnight train passenger services are still locomotive-hauled, and the West Coast route carries a higher proportion of night than day traffic, including all sleeping cars between London and points North. Shortly before our 'Day', BR had re-arranged sleepers, firstly by cutting out the East Coast service and leaving Newcastle-upon-Tyne off the sleeper map; and secondly, by slightly slowing some services to give travellers a longer and smoother night.

Those who live within sound of the West Coast main line would hardly know how much quieter the rest of BR has become at night. The great stations such as Preston and Carlisle still have a nocturnal activity reflecting patterns established in the last century. And despite today's high speeds there is still a nocturnal bottleneck over Shap; sleeping cars to London, the cross-country sleeper from Scotland to the South West, trains carrying seating passengers such as the Night Rider, the Travelling Post Office, and all types of freight still skirt the Lake District in rapid procession in the small hours. Our chosen day also still saw the time-honoured newspaper trains, though shorter than formerly, since already the delivery of many newspapers had been transferred to road, leading to the total cessation of newspaper traffic a few weeks later.

It is, of course, a much smaller BR that is kept active at night. Many routes that once carried the nation's coal, beer and food, such as the Somerset & Dorset between Bath and Templecombe, have been totally closed. Ironically, other routes which were busy by night when signal boxes had to be manned every few miles, see their automatic signals remain almost continuously at green.

By 05.00 there is already evidence of that greatest of post-war changes in the habits of business travellers: the earlier start. In Great Western

BR's Victoria to Gatwick airport shuttle service is managed by InterCity and runs every 30 minutes offering outstanding service to air travellers to and from this busy airport. The trains are run as a 'push-pull' service whereby the locomotive hauls the train to Gatwick and propels it to London Victoria. The service illustrated here is seen nearing Gatwick hauled by No 73201 *Broadlands*. (*Photo. N. J. Joynson*)

Cogload Junction is situated in the West Country and is the junction of the Bristol-Taunton line with the London-Taunton line. Heading a Speedlink working to Westbury are two of BR's Network SouthEast class 50 locomotives known to enthusiasts as 'Hoovers'! (*Photo. B. S. Dean*)

On April 14, 1988, the industrial giant, ICI Ltd held a special ceremony to mark the completion of a £44m programme to convert its own power station at Wilton on Teesside to coal firing, replacing oil. ICI's power station is the largest privately-owned power station in the country. Two computer controlled boilers consume 460,000 tonnes of coal annually. Much of this coal comes from Butterwell Colliery and this picture shows one of the Railfreight Coal sub-sector class 56 locomotives *Blyth Power*, recently adorned in the new Railfreight triple grey livery, heading a rake of empty HAA coal hoppers from Wilton to Tees Yard for onward shipment to the colliery. (*Photo Dave Hudspeth*)

days you could not pay a day visit from Cornwall to London since the last train home left Paddington before the first one up arrived.

Now the Golden Hind, with its 05.19 departure from Penzance, typifies a new breed of premium business trains to London that roll out of the depots from 04.00 onward. And though many start carrying only handfuls of passengers most are over-used in total, the serving of breakfast confined to first-class passengers. More breakfasts are served than all other restaurant car meals together and where several carfuls are fed simultaneously on the final dash to London there is much preparation work, started hours before, some crew members beavering away before any advertised food served is available.

Even some of the remaining branch lines start their passenger services earlier in the morning than used to be the case, although by last summer the writing was already on the wall for the first trip each way on the Barnstaple line. Would BR continue to run the train after the newspaper traffic was withdrawn? We now know that it did not . . . another small example of how the loss of one traffic leads to further curtailments. Indeed, almost wherever one goes at night off the West Coast main line one is shocked by the under-utilisation of the railway. Just about everybody agrees it would be more sensible to send freight by rail by night than have it clog our highways mainly by day. But things everybody agrees are desirable do not happen.

Long distance expresses start arriving in London from a wide variety of destinations almost literally hours earlier than was the case even at the beginning of the diesel and electric age. Once it was only manual workers and artisans who felt it decent to be on the rails before 07.00. Now there is no visual difference between business travellers at almost any time of day. First-class usage is indeed high in the early hours. Indeed, such is the demand for travel to London that most HSTs are now stationed in the provinces and make their first trip early to the capital before they are ready to start carrying people away from London.

From 07.00 (and on many routes earlier than that) the emphasis is of course on commuter traffic, trains rolling out of the depots and odd sidings to form continuous processions into London – standing common even by seven, endemic by half past. Summer Fridays are not the busiest of days for commuters, or for that matter the long-distance business trains into the capital. So on our day, some commuters who normally have to stand were given a reasonably comfortable journey, though staff shortages

One of the longest oil tanker trains to run daily is the Lindsey Oil Refinery (Immingham)–Colwick Junction (Nottingham) service which travels via Grantham. Eleven tankers are usually conveyed on this service which returns empty from Colwick Junction at 10.31. The return service is pictured at Melton Ross Crossing, east of Barnetby, Humberside. The hauling locomotive is class 47 No 47319 *Norsk Hydro*. (*Photo John Tuffs*)

(increased by railwaymen on holiday, or just taking an extra day off) led to the usual rash of cancellations – each a small irritant to handfuls and sometimes hundreds of people, yet hardly noticed in the overall scheme of affairs. A couple of locals from Gidea Park cancelled, poor timekeeping with Charing Cross, the usual one-off problems at Waterloo . . . nothing to write home about.

Commuting of course is not only into and out of London, but the contrast between the Network SouthEast and the other commuting systems continues to grow. Manchester, Leeds, Glasgow and others have their distinct peak patterns but never the guaranteed overcrowding of full-length formations following at minimum headways that is universal on most South Eastern lines.

Not that passengers in the Leeds area inconvenienced by stock shortages (many Pacers out of service) would have been in a mood to

There is an on-going stream of locomotives being transferred officially between depots to cater for traffic requirements or to provide locomotives of a certain type which may have a particular function, such as slow speed control. In this view, No 20146 is hauling a No 37377 which was en route from Eastfield, Glasgow, to its new home at Immingham. Sister class 20 No 20185 was also in the convoy. Transfers are most frequent at the timetable changes in May and in October when there are usually wholesale movements taking place to concentrate locomotives at a specific depot for their rostered duties. (*Photo John Tuffs*)

consider themselves fortunate. Throughout Britain road congestion helps swell BR's peak pressure; it is felt even between Exmouth and Exeter, among the branches to sport a commuters' express. The timetable still yields a fascinating crop of one-offs. For example, years ago BR maps started including a small arrow to indicate a route carrying passengers in one direction only, and in 1988 the 06.47 from Markinch for Glenrothes remained the only train to make the link from the Aberdeen main line to the Cardenden line (alas we do not have the passenger count!). What we do know is that it being school holidays the new Sprinters carried only a handful of workers over the estuary to Barmouth where the mixture of Great Western and London & Midland semaphores had only weeks to last before the Cambrian Coast conversion to radio signalling.

All go during the rush hour, trains racing smoothly past the spot on the old South Western's approach to Clapham Junction where, by the end of the year, three trains would be entwined in early morning mayhem. After rush hour the usual dozens of trains are taken out of action. These days all the London termini see the vast majority even of long-distance trains turn-round including being cleaned and relabelled in the platform, but after rush hour there is still the familiar queuing such as at Paddington through the cleaning plant down to the carriage sidings.

Our day must have been one of BR's most profitable passengerwise in 1988. Throughout the country thousands of people, who had hoped to travel on a Saver ticket cheaper on another day, knew that by leaving it to Friday they would face the higher 'White' ticket. And thousands more not so familiar with BR's charging system found their tickets more expensive than they had bargained for (booking clerks must hate Fridays and especially summer Fridays) or had to stump up extra on the return journey if using a Blue Saver. 'But nobody told me' is an argument heard increasingly often since more stations have become open, but is no excuse . . . it just makes Fridays harder for travelling ticket collectors too, especially busy summer Fridays like ours. It is, of course, only relatively recently that you paid the higher fare if you returned on a Friday as opposed to just making your outward journey then. It gives nostalgic shine to the monthly returns, a penny a mile any train any day, unlimited break of journey, of the grouping era. But then the very essence of marketing, in the air or on the rails, is to ensure that sitting in close proximity to each other you carry passengers who have paid a whole variety of fares. 'Absolutely mad, it is,' was a sentiment repeated

Throughout the system, BR runs numerous Friday-only trains to cater for the exodus of people from the conurbations escaping for the weekend. One such train is the 16.00 Reading–York service. This is a surprising route, but in effect incorporates two trains – a Reading– Birmingham service and a Birmingham–York service. (The quickest way from Reading to York is, in fact, via London and down the East Coast main line to York!) Class 47 No 47654 *Finsbury Park* powers the train into Derby station. (*Photo John Tuffs*)

hundreds of times this busy Friday, but the truth is it is good marketing and makes money. Even with the discouragement of the higher Saver rate, most expresses on all major routes were well filled, some embarrassingly so. I had to stand all the way from Newton Abbot . . . not a spare seat even after Exeter!

The middle of the day, 10.00 to 16.00, is when BR looks its best . . . a rich diversity of types of railway, many wearing their historic origins lightly on their sleeve, running through every type of terrain, signalled by upper and lower quadrants and electric light signals, the trains powered by an incredible variety of diesel and electric engines. Smaller, less varied, possibly less glamorous than it used to be; yes. Dull; certainly not. Despite it being generally a rather grey day, the spotters were out in force, recording train times, engine names and numbers, even the formation of individual trains coach number by coach number, enjoying the holiday feeling that grew as the day progressed. The famous trains such as the Flying Scotsman and Cornish Riviera, only standard HSTs though they may be, handsomely earned their keep on schedules that nobody dreamt of thirty years ago. Exeter in two hours! Bath by the West Country Pullman (in its first season) non-stop from Paddington at BR's highest start-to-stop speed, a steady ton plus, luxury snacks for the first-class passengers in the so-called Pullmans.

Fridays, generally are poor days for specifically first-class, business travel. Another change in the pattern of business travel is that while people start their working days earlier, they also finish sooner – both the individual day and especially the working week. Once trains leaving London at up to seven on Friday evenings were the week's busiest. Now restaurant cars and most first-class cars see more passengers on Thursday

Surveyors are not just found with estate agents. BR has a large number of such personnel engaged on many civil engineering duties. This one was at work at Melton Ross Crossing near Barnetby. He is very naughty – he is not wearing a high visibility jacket! (*Photo John Tuffs*)

At 02.30, a High Speed Train power car eases through the washing plant at St Philips Marsh depot, Bristol. The depot services ten HST sets throughout each night (the total operated by the Western Region is 38) and is one of four servicing depots, the others being at Old Oak Common depot, London, Laira depot, Plymouth and Long Rock depot, Penzance. (*Photo Mike Goodfield*)

Commuters pay many hundreds of pounds to park their motors. At 07.50, this commuter at Huntingdon grabs his latest ticket before heading for London. (*Photo Gordon Bird*)

Refineries at Thames Haven, Immingham, Stanlow, Milford Haven and Grangemouth provide much business for Railfreight's Petroleum sub-sector. There is a constant procession of loaded trains from, and empty trains to, these terminals. This train is conveying empty 4-wheeled tanks known as type TTA to Lindsey, Immingham, ready to be loaded. A class 31 locomotive No 31403 is providing the traction and the location is Barnetby. (*Photo John Tuffs*)

rather than Friday evenings, and the peak rush so far as long-distance traffic is concerned is closer to 16.30 than 18.30 on Fridays. Even commuters start home earlier on Fridays, and in rather smaller numbers since more routines are broken at the beginning of the weekend. The very worst road traffic jams tend to be after tea time on Fridays when generally BR holds its head high.

As far as *second-class* railway travel is concerned, especially in summer, by lunch time at any major station you can tell when it is Friday. More people are carrying heavy luggage, clothes are fresh, even flowers more common (in buttonhole or by the bunch for friends). Many routes still have extra Friday afternoon and early evening trains, or see formations lengthened. On several routes such as down to the West, even the more expensive white Savers are banned on the regular HSTs and those wishing to use them forced to travel on 'horse-and-coaches' older stock, including compartments which indeed some older passengers can still be seen savouring each Friday.

King's Cross sports a kind of Friday test of nerves as far more passengers present themselves for train upon train than can comfortably be accommodated. First class fills up here because it is the only way many people can hope to get a seat. The West Coast main line which has slipped so badly down the league table in the past two decades at least shows what the flexibility of locomotive-hauled stock can achieve, though conversely its first class is less resorted to by the economy-minded weekend brigade.

Booking offices, refreshment rooms, trains . . . if all were kept as busy the rest of the week as on Fridays, BR would surely be highly profitable. Down to the coast in Wales or to Whitby, on the Glasgow suburban service, or on the cross-country main line from through Sheffield and Birmingham to Bristol, the extra business is welcome and makes the railway itself seem worthwhile. But extra passengers take longer to get on and off, and summer Fridays are certainly not the best days for punctuality. It generally starts well and deteriorates . . . and yet again

March depot is the location of many withdrawn locomotives waiting for the breaker's yard. This desolate scene was taken at 06.20. Locomotives are towed to this location from as far away as Sheffield for storage pending sale or removal of components for further use. (*Photo Gordon Bird*)

BR's Speedlink network, which in October of 1988 was merged with Freightliners, has a core network of main yards from which the high speed air-braked trains operate. One of these yards is at Doncaster Belmont and it was to this location that this Speedlink trip was proceeding for onward transhipment – the 15.25 Immingham Norsk Hydro to Doncaster conveying Hydro fertiliser wagons. Class 47 No 47295 is the locomotive, pictured near Barnetby. (*Photo John Tuffs*)

Unglamorous, but lucrative and necessary are the many parcels trains run daily for the Post Office. Locomotive No 31443 arrives at Derby in charge of the 16.08 London St Pancras–Leeds parcels. (*Photo John Tuffs*)

the Western Region succeeded in carrying passengers far more expeditiously to Paddington than it seemed capable of returning them, down trains at Exeter St David's losing their customary extra minutes.

Later Friday evenings are a peculiar time. Throughout the provinces, knots of people wait for the train that will bring their loved-ones or friends for the weekend or start of holiday. Mainly people who rarely travel by train themselves, they must have a jaundiced view of BR as they hang around for late-running second-rate trains. Station approaches are usually congested, and many have to park irregularly (how do you limit your parking to twenty minutes if the train you are meeting is thirty minutes late?) to avoid going into the paying areas of car parks whose charges are geared to business men leaving their vehicles for whole days. Many of the stations at which these people wait are more or less deserted until an express runs in from London or some other major centre. Then all hell breaks loose for a few minutes, followed by another deathly silence. Railmen are increasingly conspicuous by their absence on Friday evenings; even station announcements seem scantier as though those making them had caught the weekend spirit.

Kisses put all complaints of BR (indeed BR's very existence) out of mind. But then among a group of a hundred or so waiters there will always be one whose passenger does not turn up. What agonies of thought! It is more usually a misunderstanding than a late connection, though sometimes a change of train because of Saver-linked restrictions. So to save £5, daughter keeps rich mum or dad waiting an hour they'd have paid £50 to avoid!

Meantime the suburban lines go quiet. Friday evening is car time even for people who leave their vehicle in the garage from Mondays to Thursdays. Shopping and social time. Eating out and theatre time, too, and in larger cities and certainly London that still means train. But even when it is not exactly slack, suburban business is erratic, unprofitable. Throughout the country much of the profit BR has earned during the day is lost in evening, especially Friday evening, as social demands still win over crude commerce. What business run strictly as a business would shuttle a diesel multiple unit even between Newton Abbot and Paignton for a dozen to a score of passengers?

It is now, perhaps, that one realises more than at any other time just how much traffic has left the rails. Evenings were the time of the milk trains, the fruit, vegetable and flower trains. Once the railway was part

Now here's a novelty – loading the refreshment trolley with passenger assistance! BR Network SouthEast provides a trolley service with private caterers on the electric multiple-unit services on the Great Northern main line between King's Cross and Huntingdon where this picture was taken at 08.05. (*Photo Gordon Bird*)

of the countryside through which it ran; such parcels and freights now running are not from agrarian but chemical, oil, industrial and above all quarry Britain. As already mentioned, on our particular Friday newspapers were still being sent by train, from Manchester as well as London; but there is another class of business since lost. Even parcels offices are mainly closed in the evenings, and indeed when open no longer deal in volume but with odds and bits, especially Red Star. The farmer whose products may now never travel by train may still depend on Red Star to bring a badly-needed spare part for a machine for the weekend harvest. There is indeed a new kind of PLA (passenger luggage in advance); not the railway collecting your holiday luggage from your home and delivering it to boarding house to allow you to travel light but groups of people who fill cars so full that some baggage has to be sent by train. And some of those waiting to meet passenger trains on Friday evenings have made the journey down by car earlier themselves. The railway still provides much such social service . . . the odds and sods, the overflows, that people who normally take themselves everywhere cannot cope with, the social railway epitomised by the Fridays-only Norwich–North

One of BR's valuable contracts is that to convey imported iron ore from Immingham to the steel plants at BSC Scunthorpe. Many thousands of tonnes of ore are carried annually in a slick operation using two class 37 locomotives and specially converted hopper wagons which once worked on the Tyne Dock–Consett ore trains. A loaded train is depicted in full cry passing Barnetby en route to the Santon terminal at Scunthorpe. The locomotives are based at Immingham depot for this duty and two of these, Nos 37225 and 37083 are seen in action. (*Photo John Tuffs*)

British Rail has two test tracks. One is at Old Dalby in Leicestershire and the other is near Derby at Mickleover. These are used to try out equipment and trains. One of BR's Research Department's test trains is the Tribometer Train which measures surface resistance between wheels and the rail. It is frequently seen around the country, but on the day in question was actually in use at Mickleover. This view shows the brightly coloured train being propelled along the Mickleover to Eggington Junction test track in connection with paper tape contamination tests. The vehicles are railway laboratories and are fitted out with sensitive measuring equipment and computer technology. (*Photos John Tuffs*)

Another of the Research Department's test trains was out on the day under review. This train was returning one of the Test Cars, Mentor, (second coach from the locomotive) to the Railway Technical Centre at Derby. The train is passing Offord on the Great Northern main line and the locomotive is No 47480 *Robin Hood*, one of two class 47 locomotives allocated to the Research Department. (*Photo Gordon Bird*)

History starts yesterday, someone once said and this picture is already history. In the summer of 1988 the Carlisle–Glasgow Central service was still locomotive hauled, but with the October timetable change, this route went over to Sprinter operation. No 47341, a Railfreight sector locomotive, heads the 14.00 Carlisle–Glasgow service at New Cumnock. (*Photo Paul D. Shannon*)

One of the long running (literally) freight trains is the daily Clitheroe–Gunnie (Glasgow) cement train, which takes loaded cement hoppers from Castle Cement's works via the West Coast main line to Scotland. This train at one time ran via the Settle & Carlisle line but now runs the longer way round to Carlisle. Two Scottish based class 37 locomotives are rostered for this service and this picture shows the train running nearly two hours early at Abingdon powered by class 37 Nos 37160 and 37127. (*Photo Paul D. Shannon*)

Walsham carrying one or two weekenders from London (a departure two hours later than possible other days) along with a few on strictly local journeys. Until recently there was a Fridays-only through to Sheringham. How much longer will anything run down this erstwhile main line after 22.00?

Overcrowded during the peaks, under-used much of the evening, BR winds down. Restaurant car stewards pay in their day's takings, drivers report faults, the level of activity at HST maintenance depots mounts again . . . and a few thousand people prepare to spend the night on the rails. Summer Friday evenings still see the departure of overnight holiday expresses, such as that caught by our reporter who writes 'One Traveller's Day' in later pages. Furthermore, most sleepers are booked solid. It was businessmen during the week. Now the need is for twin berths for husbands and wives and family parties. However hard they work during the week, businessmen feel hard done by if they are not home till Saturday morning.

A typical day. Too many passengers here, too few there; some profitable bulk freights, but not nearly enough; despite a Pullman special from Llandrindod Wells, the social railway such as the Central Wales line (truncated a few months before by its fatal bridge collapse in a flood) saps the vitality of the vibrant main lines. The main lines that are increasingly road, as opposed to branch line, fed. Mechanical failures, the usual post-mortems, an army of administrators grappling with paperwork (though perhaps only one in ten of those were around thirty years ago, when the definition of 'railway' was more a source of employment than a means of transport). No doubt somewhere a further small parcel of former railway land was sold back to the community by the Property Board. In some offices the week ended with decisions on more economies.

Much friendliness from railwaymen, many of whom went well beyond the normal course of duty to help their customers; but also the usual disgruntled, 'I don't make the rules', and change of restaurant car and Pullman service without adequate reason ('we know our rights'). Examine it in detail and running BR even for a day amounts to a more formidable management challenge than that presented to any company in the 'private sector'. At least in the summer of 1988 it was still felt that BR would remain BR, though the subsequent talk of options in privatisation would not have come as a surprise. The surprise now is no change, continuity. Once railwaymen were in a predictable industry; no longer. On our summer Friday, as on any other day, it shows.

One of Railfreight's most successful operations is the conveyance of imported iron ore from Hunterston on the River Clyde to British Steel Motherwell. The trains run on a 'merry-go-round' principle whereby the locomotives (Motherwell based class 37s) remain with their tippler wagons throughout the day. Some of the most arduous locomotive work in the country is required from these machines as they take their trains, each weighing 1,575 tonnes, to Ravenscraig, Motherwell before returning the empties to Hunterston. Here Nos 37320 and 37049 are in full cry at Steventson with a Ravenscraig-bound train. (*Photo Paul D. Shannon*)

'Thank you, madam'. Ticket inspection at Huntingdon at 08.00. (*Photo Gordon Bird*)

Another area of the country which sees an intensive iron ore service operated to the blast furnace is in South Wales. Iron ore is imported from Port Talbot and taken to the Llanwern steelworks using pairs of class 56 locomotives, again in a merry-go-round type service. The locomotives never leave their hopper wagons which are filled and unloaded still coupled to the traction. In full cry, Nos 56055 and 56040 pass Pengam with one of the numerous daily services which ply to and from Llanwern. (*Photo Michael Rhodes*)

Assistant Station Manager, Mr Black, provides assistance to a traveller at Bristol Temple Meads station, one of the most magnificent stations in the British Isles. (*Photo Mike Goodfield*)

Remember the 'Blue Trains' of Glasgow which ushered out the steam trains on the local suburban system in the early 1960s? Some of these vintage electric trains are still running. They were later designated class 303 and this unit, No 303091, is seen at Springburn having arrived from Milngavie. Passengers can change here to catch the Diesel Multiple Unit (DMU) for the 16-minute journey to Cumbernauld. (*Photo Tom Noble*)

THE RAILFREIGHT SCENE

Railfreight today is a thriving business. BR has finally shaken off the time-honoured image of slow, loose-coupled goods trains and huge sprawling marshalling yards, and offers an increasingly efficient and streamlined service for the conveyance of bulk freight. To the enthusiast and general observer of the railway scene, however, the negative aspects of the Railfreight metamorphosis may be more readily apparent than the positive ones. The regular rail traveller cannot fail to notice the derelict sidings and deserted marshalling yards which often remain by the lineside as a reminder of 'more prosperous' times. Those yards that remain open often seem half empty, and the trains themselves seem fewer and further between than they were in bygone days. A good number of freight-only lines have succumbed to the axe in the last decade or so, just as the Beeching era saw the demise of much of the secondary passenger network. To those who remember the steady stream of coal trains rattling over Woodhead or the hive of activity (lasting well into the 1980s) at Severn Tunnel Junction marshalling yard, today's freight railway seems but a shadow of its former self.

True, some traffic flows have been lost in recent years from rail to road, especially where low or irregular tonnages and short distances made the railway uncompetitive. However, such losses have been compensated for by growth in key areas such as roadstone and coal, bulk commodities for which the railway is excellently suited. Paradoxically, it is the derelict marshalling yards and closed goods depots which betray the secret of

Besides the main Speedlink workings, there are many 'trip' workings taking vehicles from and to the main Speedlink yards where they are marshalled for onward transhipment. One of these trains is depicted here – the 6T19 Mossend Giffen trip freight. The train is seen at Lugton on the Glasgow–Kilmarnock line where the locomotive, No 37251, has just left ten open wagons loaded with fertiliser in the sidings on the right of the picture. The remaining vehicles on the train are loaded with military stores. (*Photo Paul D. Shannon*)

British Rail secures much business from the transport of incoming goods to this country, ranging from fruit, Perrier water, coal and steel. This latter commodity is represented in this picture showing a train of imported billets which had arrived by ship at Hamworthy, Poole, arriving at its destination of Tidal Yard, Cardiff. No 47142 provides the power. (*Photo Michael Rhodes*)

The Freightliner terminal at Cardiff is situated at Pengam from which Freightliner services serve many destinations throughout the country. Freightliners, until October 1988, was a wholly owned subsidiary of the British Railways Board, but from this date was merged with Speedlink to form a new concern – Railfreight Distribution. Another class 47 No 47123 shunts at Pengam, marshalling the Pengam–Stratford, East London, service. Previously, this train ran from Danycraig, Swansea. (*Photo Michael Rhodes*)

Tidal Yard is a main sorting yard for Cardiff rail freight. It sees a variety of traffic ranging from general produce, coal, and steel which abound in plentiful quantities in this part of the country. Winding its way out of the yard is the 16.50 Speedlink service to Mossend, Glasgow, headed by a class 47 machine No 47214. On the day in question, the train conveyed 15 wagons with steel from Associated Wire & Steel in Cardiff to Mossend and Stranraer. At Hereford, a further nine wagons of cider and timber would be attached for the journey to Scotland. (*Photo Michael Rhodes*)

A considerable quantity of coal is imported into Scotland and one of the locations where this occurs is at Rothesay Dock, Clydebank. In this view a pair of class 26 locomotives prepare to move the latest load to Kincardine power station. (*Photo Tom Noble*)

Railfreight's success as a self-supporting and profitable business in the late 1980s. Whilst the overall tonnage of freight on BR has remained roughly constant in the last five years, BR's costs per train-mile have been reduced by a remarkable 20% in the same period. Irretrievably uneconomic freight flows have been discarded, and any superfluous resources – whether these be locomotives, wagons, sidings or lines – have progressively been weeded out, leaving a tightly controlled system where every Railfreight asset must earn its keep.

Looming large in any review of Railfreight in the 1980s must be the phenomenon of 'sectorisation', that is to say the division of BR into a number of distinct 'businesses' for accounting and administration purposes. Each of the five sectors may in turn be split into sub-sectors, and in the case of the Railfreight sector this has led to the setting up of separate organisations for Coal, Construction, Petroleum, Metals

Commuters at Huntingdon (58 miles from London) prepare to board the 08.31 service to King's Cross (06.12 from Cleethorpes) but they may well be unlikely to get a seat on this popular train. (*Photo Gordon Bird*)

(formerly Metals/Automotive) and Distribution businesses. The effects of sectorisation on the network have been far-reaching and profound, for wherever possible all costs incurred in running the railway must be assigned to a specific area of the business, whether these be the costs of running and managing the trains or the costs of maintaining and modernising the infrastructure. No longer do the majority of funds come from an anonymous 'common purse'. So if no sector or sub-sector will sponsor a particular locomotive class, for example, or a particular maintenance depot, then its future is immediately threatened. Similarly, on the positive side, the impetus for major projects such as a line reopening is likely to come from one particular sub-sector; a striking example of this in 1987 was the Mauchline–Annbank reopening, funded wholly by Railfreight Coal.

The Railfreight organisation is, understandably, keen to project a positive image of itself to present day and prospective customers. In

BR ScotRail operates an outstanding half-hourly service between Edinburgh and Glasgow using the 'push-pull' system whereby the locomotive hauls the train one way and pushes the train in the reverse direction, controlled by a driver sitting in a driving brake coach at the end of the train. One of the special locomotives dedicated for this service and also others in Scotland which use the 'push-pull' mode, No 47710, climbs Cowlairs Bank out of Glasgow Queen Street station with the 09.00 to Edinburgh. This section of track is reversibly signalled, which permits trains to use either track in either direction – one at a time, of course! (*Photo Tom Noble*)

One of the driving brake coaches used on 'push-pull' trains is seen here at Edinburgh Waverley. The coach is part of the 12.30 service from Glasgow. GPO staff unload mail. The cowcatcher can be seen below the bufferbeam and it is sad to relate that it was a cow which caused a serious accident to one of these trains at Polmont and which brought about the fitting of cowcatchers to all the fleet of these driving brake coaches. (*Photo Tom Noble*)

February 1987, a design policy statement was issued by the British Railways Board, emphasising the importance of Railfreight's image as an outward indication of its optimism and dynamism as a business. The most conspicuous change was to be one of locomotive livery; the Railfreight grey adopted in the mid 1980s with the arrival of the class 58 was now considered to be too dull and nondescript, and so a new set of house colours was devised. A ceremony at Ripple Lane depot on October 15, 1987 first brought the new scheme into public view, with representatives of classes 37, 47, 56 and 58 each sporting two-tone grey sides, dark grey roof, bodyside sub-sector logo and cabside depot badge. The new Railfreight 'identity' is being applied not only to locomotives but also where appropriate to wagons, external direction signs, publicity material and even headed notepaper. As one might expect with any innovation, opinions have been divided as to the appropriateness and attractiveness of the new Railfreight livery. The scheme has won the accolade of

inclusion in the 1988 *Design and Arts Directors* publication, whereas its opponents have condemned the results as gaudy or gimmicky. From the enthusiast's point of view, the new colours are at the very least a source of variation on an otherwise increasingly standardised locomotive fleet.

Railfreight's biggest source of traffic is coal, running at the rate of approximately 75 million tonnes per annum. Pit closures and general industrial decline have certainly taken their toll in recent decades, but the business has recovered well since the miners' strike of 1984/5 and BR has actually increased its market share of the commodity during the last few years. The majority of coal trains follow the highly successful 'merry-go-round' concept, where a fixed formation of locomotive and wagons operates a 'circuit' from colliery to power station and back without the need for remarshalling en route. At most modern power stations, discharge can be effected whilst the train remains in motion, so that a turn-round time of minutes rather than hours is possible. Many collieries

Signalman Stuart Driver at work in the small signalbox at Derby Road, on the Ipswich–Felixstowe branch. This line has a local passenger service but is also a main freight route with many Freightliner services daily. (*Photo John Day*)

Driver Gooch of Parkeston Quay, Harwich, receives the single line token from Signalman Driver to proceed from Derby Road to Trimley, then on to Felixstowe South Freightliner Terminal. The two class 37 locomotives, Nos 37178 and 37107 will then work the 10.22 service to Garston Freightliner terminal at Liverpool. (*Photo John Day*)

Meanwhile, at the next box at Trimley, a similar procedure is enacted later in the day between Signalman Allan Peck who hands over the single line token to Driver Gooch working the 10.22 Felixstowe South–Garston Freightliner service. The little boy begins his dream of becoming a train driver! (*Photo John Day*)

and opencast sites are now similarly equipped with a rapid loading bunker, in order to provide an equal level of efficiency at the other end of the process.

Merry-go-round services operate in many parts of the country, but the most concentrated operations are those in the Trent Valley (serving the CEGB at Ratcliffe, High Marnham, Cottam, West Burton and three smaller locations) and the Aire Valley (serving the CEGB at Drax, Eggborough and Ferrybridge). Other major power stations receiving coal by merry-go-round services are Aberthaw, Didcot, Ironbridge, Rugeley, Thorpe Marsh, Fidlers Ferry, Blyth, Cockenzie and Longannet. Some coal trains supply fuel to other industrial users, such as British Steel at Llanwern, Bowaters at Sittingbourne and ICI at Wilton, and BR carries coal for export and import through ports as diverse as Ayr, Swansea (both exports), Hunterston and King's Lynn (both imports). For the domestic market and for a few smaller industrial concerns, BR also operates a fast wagonload network, marketed as Speedlink Coal, linking approximately 25 collieries and patent fuel plants with roughly 35 concentration depots up and down the country. A major innovation in the 1980s has been the use of containers for some domestic coal traffic, enabling door-to-door transit of a commodity which is surprisingly susceptible to damage during handling. Trainload container services run from the North East and from South Wales to Ellesmere Port for shipment to Ireland, and also from

Every Friday, a long distance train sets off from Newcastle to Cardiff – the 17.10 departure. It is unusual because it still comprises old Mark 1 coaching stock. There are some passengers who would despair having to ride such distances in 30-year-old vehicles, but, equally so, there are many rail enthusiasts who would relish the chance to travel in 'real' coaches behind a locomotive – a fast diminishing aspect of passenger travel in the British Isles. No 47625 was rostered for this duty when pictured at Low Fell, just south of Newcastle, on this particular Friday evening. (*Photo Neville E. Stead*)

Glasgow Central station has deservedly earned the highest praise for the way it has been so beautifully restored to cater for a modern railway, but yet has retained so much of its historic character. The old and the new are pictured blended in this view and illustrate how this and so many more terminal stations have become shopping centres as well as their true role. (*Photo Tom Noble*)

No *Day in the Life of BR* book would be complete without this scene enacted thousands of times daily throughout the whole system. This one is the last kiss before the London train pulls out of Glasgow Central. It was at the start of the Glasgow holiday fortnight and was one of several special trains put on to cater for the annual exodus. (*Photo Tom Noble*)

Felixstowe North Freightliner Terminal at 10.00. On the left is the previous night's 20.07 service from Glasgow Coatbridge headed by class 47 No 47515 *Night Mail*. On the right can be seen the 10.18 service to London, Willesden, conveying traffic for Manchester and Liverpool. This train is headed by class 37 Nos 37128 and 37010. (*Photo John Day*)

The only activity at Dover Priory at lunchtime was the arrival of a parcels unit, No 9004. These Driving Motor Luggage Vans (DMLVs) operate on behalf of the Post Office and some of the fleet are now being painted in the PO's red livery. (*Photo Paul Savage*)

Concentration is the order of the day for Senior Railman, Bob Sharpe, at Colwyn Bay on the North Wales Coast line. 'The train now arriving at platform 1 is the 15.11 for Holyhead'. (*Photo Larry Goddard*)

Victoria station has always been the gateway to Europe, although with the coming of the Channel Tunnel, this accolade will pass to Waterloo station. This will become, initially, the main terminal for European traffic, followed later by a new underground station at King's Cross. A varied and cosmopolitan section of humanity can be viewed daily at Victoria where signs for Paris, Milan and Frankfurt vie for attention with Ramsgate and Brighton. (*Photo Paul Savage*)

South Wales pits to Swansea Docks, whilst several inland concentration depots (mostly in Scotland) receive smaller consignments of containerised coal via the Speedlink network.

The Railfreight Construction sub-sector deals primarily with aggregates for road building, but also handles a variety of other products such as cement, bricks, tiles and even household refuse. The aggregates traffic comprises some 14 million tonnes a year, of which nearly three-quarters is destined for construction markets in London and the South East. Trainloads of roadstone run to this part of the country from Merehead, Whatley and Tytherington in the west and also from various sites in the Midlands, including Croft, Bardon Hill, Cliffe Hill, Mountsorrel (all Leicestershire) and Peak Forest. Competition between roadstone suppliers is vigorous and it is not uncommon to find several companies' discharge terminals within a few miles of each other, such as Acton (Foster Yeoman), West Drayton (ARC), Hayes & Harlington (Tarmac) and Thorney Mill (Bardon) all in West London. One of the Foster Yeoman trains from Merehead, a nightly service to Purfleet, is now Britain's heaviest train, regularly loading to 4,700 tonnes between Merehead and Acton. Such is the South East's insatiable demand for stone that the coming years are likely to see further increases in the annual tonnage conveyed by rail. Cement, bricks and tiles are conveyed in a mixture of block trains and individual wagon loads, whilst containerised household refuse is carried by block train from three sites in London, four in Manchester and three in Avon.

Under the banner of Railfreight Petroleum, BR is presently carrying just over 10 million tonnes of oil and oil-related products per annum. There is a small amount of home-produced crude oil, mainly from Furzebrook (Dorset), Holybourne (Hampshire) and Welton (Lincolnshire), but the greater part of the traffic is made up of refined products such as fuel oil, heating oil, bitumen and liquid petroleum gas. These products are forwarded from refineries at Stanlow, Grangemouth, Immingham (two), Thames Haven (two), Robeston, Waterston, Llandarcy, Fawley, Port Clarence and Harwich, and also from several storage depots such as Bowling (Clydeside), Grain (Kent) and Bromford Bridge (Birmingham). Most of the Petroleum sub-sector's traffic is carried in block trains of 46-tonne and/or 102-tonne tanks, running direct from refineries to specialised discharge terminals in many parts of the country. Wagonload traffic is largely restricted to BR's traction fuel supplies,

Few of the general public have much knowledge of what a station telephone inquiry office looks like. This one is at Newcastle. Soon all major stations will be equipped with a computer system which, with the keying in of abbreviated station names with dates will, in just a few seconds, provide a list of train connections, thus relieving the operator from manually searching timetables. Clever stuff! (*Photo Robin Trinder*)

One of numerous Boat Trains operated by BR daily to connect with important sailings, the 13.05 Holyhead–Euston Boat Train, runs through Colwyn Bay powered by No 47453. (*Photo Larry Goddard*)

certain flows from Grangemouth to the Highlands of Scotland, and bitumen from Thames Haven, Fawley and Ellesmere Port. The traffic as a whole has been in decline since the early 1970s, partly due to sinking demand but also due to the construction of pipelines on several major routes, eg Fawley to Birmingham. At the time of writing, however, the prospects for growth in Railfreight Petroleum were looking good, as evidenced by this sub-sector's keen interest in securing some of the first of the new order of class 60 heavy freight locomotives.

Steel is the main commodity handled by the Metals subsector. Changes in rail traffic patterns in the last decade or so have been considerable, reflecting the drastic changes effected in the steel industry itself. But BR continues to carry a sizeable share of the available traffic, especially in the initial stages of the steel-making process. Imported iron ore is carried from Hunterston to Ravenscraig, from Immingham to Scunthorpe and

The driver of a Largs-bound train prepares to board his train for another run at Glasgow Central. These new electric trains, designated class 318 and built by British Rail Engineering Ltd, York, commenced operation in 1987 and have transformed the standard of service between Glasgow and Ayr and Largs. Previously, the service was operated by an extraordinary collection of vintage, life-expired, diesel multiple units which gained a notorious reputation. (*Photo Tom Noble*)

Every day, Ketton Cement works situated near Stamford on the Peterborough to Leicester line despatches a loaded train to the Midlands. A curiosity of this train is that, because of the track layout at Ketton, the train has no course but to run in the wrong direction to Peterborough where the locomotive runs round its train before setting off to its destination actually passing Ketton en route! It would cost too much to install run-round facilities at Ketton and hence this amusing anachronism continues. The loaded train is pictured leaving Peterborough, having already traversed the track on the left. (*Photo John Rudd*)

from Port Talbot to Llanwern, all in semi-permanently coupled rakes of 100-tonne tippler wagons. Raw steel is then sent in coiled or slab form from Ravenscraig, Lackenby, Port Talbot and Llanwern to further BSC plants such as Shotton, Corby, Ebbw Vale and Etruria, again mostly in block trains. Beyond this, traffic patterns are too complicated to be enumerated in detail. There are, however, major flows of semi-finished steel from South Yorkshire, Scunthorpe, Teesside, South Wales, Ravenscraig, Etruria and Sheerness, and scrap metal is carried by rail to South Yorkshire (Deepcar and Aldwarke), Cardiff, Clydesdale and Sheerness. International traffic is important, too, both via the Dover–Dunkerque train ferry and also through ports such as Grimsby, King's Lynn and Hamworthy. Much of the semi-finished steel and scrap traffic is conveyed by the wagonload rather than by the trainload, and some Speedlink (ie wagonload) services are sponsored by this subsector. The Automotive traffic includes motor vehicle components to and from Ford plants at Bridgend, Dagenham and Halewood, and Austin Rover plants at Longbridge, Oxford and Swindon. The finished product is conveyed from many British factories and also from foreign sources to a small number of rail-served distribution points on BR, including Bathgate, Stranraer (for Northern Ireland), Wakefield, Garston, Oxford and Exeter.

The fifth and final Railfreight sub-sector is identified by the name Distribution, and covers a very wide range of commodities falling outside the four categories discussed above. From an operational point of view, most Distribution traffic has up until recently been identified with BR's Speedlink network, since both are concerned with smaller-scale flows which would not on their own justify the running of a separate train service. Commodities range from caustic soda and wood pulp to Coca-Cola and whisky, and traffic between Britain and mainland Europe forms an important part of the sub-sector's business as a whole. The Speedlink network was established in the early 1980s, with a network of fast 'trunk' trains running between a limited number of strategically placed yards, and local 'trip' workings running from each yard to individual freight terminals (mainly private sidings) as and when required. The essence of the Speedlink system is overnight delivery, which is possible for all but the very longest traffic flows. Thus, a consignment of Guinness beer will leave the Park Royal factory at tea time, join a northbound Speedlink service from Willesden to Glasgow later the same evening, and be 'tripped' out to the distribution terminal outside Glasgow early the following morning. A major change was heralded for Railfreight Distribution in October, 1988, with the announcement of a merger between the existing Speedlink-based organisation and Freightliners, hitherto a wholly-owned subsidiary of the BRB. The merger is intended to improve the financial and operational performance of both groups, and will facilitate a joint onslaught on the extra international traffic which is expected to become available upon the dismantling of European trade barriers in 1992 and the opening of the Channel Tunnel in the following year. Some routes in future will probably see trains carrying both Speedlink and Freightliner traffic; indeed plans were announced immediately after the merger for a joint service between Bristol and Coatbridge.

Looking more closely at Railfreight traction, it is significant that designs for recent and forthcoming diesel locomotive types have broken away from the 1955 Modernisation Plan mould of predominantly mixed

It's a long way up! A duty performed countless times every day around the country is the refilling of the oil lamps on the semaphore signals. As colour light signalling spreads as modernisation schemes are implemented, the sight of a man up a signal will diminish. The signal gantry at the east end of Rhyl station receives attention from 'Dick the Lamp', a name bestowed on him by the railmen in best Welsh tradition. (*Photo Larry Goddard*)

A sad scene which can be seen every night at many major rail terminals. The less fortunate members of society tend to gravitate to railway stations where there is a sense of communal security. This particular incident took place at Glasgow Central at 23.45. (*Photo Tom Noble*)

'What do you make of it, Walter?' At Ipswich's Carriage & Wagon Repair Shops, Eric Proudfoot (left) and Walter Buckley examine a sheared-off buffer from a Freightliner vehicle (from an incident which took place the previous day) whilst Adrian Mitchell of Freightliners looks on. (*Photo John Day*)

A welcome innovation by InterCity in 1987 was the introduction of Sleeper Lounge coaches on the sleeper services on the West Coast main line (Euston–Glasgow). Passengers may avail themselves of refreshments prior to retiring and also obtain breakfasts upon, or near, arrival. On the selected day of this compilation, business was quiet and perhaps the photographer should have asked the young lady her name . . . (*Photo Tom Noble*)

Barry station serves a busy community and sees both passenger and freight trains. The line continues as a branch to Barry Island and also diverges to run along the coast through Aberthaw. It is from this latter place that a rake of empty coal wagons are passing through, headed by a class 37 locomotive en route to the valley collieries to refill. On the left, a Barry Island-bound multiple unit departs. Passenger and freight business in South Wales has experienced a welcome resurgence throughout 1988. (*Photo Deryck Lewis*)

traffic units. Even the existing locomotive fleet has been divided up between the sectors and sub-sectors, with Railfreight taking the responsibility for roughly 1,100 locomotives. Besides being reliveried in the house colours described earlier, each Railfreight locomotive is intended to bear the logo of its originating sub-sector and the emblem of its home maintenance depot. Most trunk Speedlink trains, for example, are powered by class 47 locomotives dedicated to the Distribution sub-sector and allocated to Tinsley depot, Sheffield; they will therefore carry the 'red diamonds' sub-sector logo and 'white rose' depot emblem. Other early examples of fleet dedication were the North Thameside petroleum class 37/7s, the Cornish china clay class 37/5s, and the South Wales Metals class 37/9s. Once a locomotive has been identified with a particular sub-sector, it does not totally preclude its use on other sub-sectors' services. Quite apart from emergencies and 'rescue' operations, traction resources in certain remoter areas (eg West Highland Line) may be shared between more than one sector for the sake of economy and efficiency.

The wagon fleet in 1989 comprises approximately 42,000 vehicles, a mere fraction of the vast pool of rolling stock which lay at BR's disposal in the 1960s and 1970s. Of these 42,000, roughly one third are privately owned, although they account for a greater proportion of traffic than the railway-owned vehicles. All petroleum and chemical tanks are privately owned, as are the majority of roadstone hoppers and other specialised vehicles. BR's own stock comprises the fleet of HAA merry-go-round coal hoppers, most steel carriers, various air-braked vans and open wagons for Speedlink flows, and an ever-declining number of outmoded vacuum-braked vehicles, mainly HTV hopper wagons. The shift to air-braked operation was begun in the 1960s and was complete except for a handful of trainload flows by the late 1980s. Ironically, it looks as if some of the last vacuum-braked survivors will be the PHV hoppers used by ICI on their Tunstead–Northwich limestone traffic; many of these wagons date back to the 1930s, although they are still in very sound condition and fit for a good few years' service yet. Looking into the future, much interest is focussed on container traffic and inter-modal systems such as Mini-Link, MaxiLink and TrailerTrain. Several new freight flows are based on the use of containers, such as Avon–Calvert refuse, Melton Mowbray–Manchester petfood and South Wales/Lynemouth–Ellesmere Port coal, and the inter-modal MiniLink system has already been operating successfully between Willesden and Deanside (Glasgow).

ONE TRAVELLER'S DAY

The day began on Newton Abbot station discussing the framed tribute to the Great Western's staff who lost their lives serving their King in the First World War; of the 25,479 employees who joined the forces, 2,436 were killed, 23 of them from Newton Abbot where until the 1950s nearly 2,000 railwaymen were employed. The last time the writer drew attention to an interesting relic on Newton Abbot station, some petty-minded official had it instantly destroyed; one of those relief maps, showing the height of mountains and how the railways threaded through the valleys, that helped entertain passengers waiting for late-running trains in bygone days.

The reason for the midnight discussion was the late-running Penzance–Paddington sleeper. The journey should have begun the previous day at 23.50, but – memories of the last trains on branch lines running so late as to keep the service going into another day – the sleeper did not arrive until well into *the* day under focus. The 13-coach formation included six sleepers, though two of them were working back to Paddington empty, no doubt for the peak of down-traffic on Friday night. The up sleeper does not have the reputation for being the safest way to travel from the West; even at the height of the GWR's safety spell between the two wars, there was a nasty crash when it ran into a goods train, while in recent years there was the notorious Taunton sleeping car fire (hopefully they do not lock the doors these days, though it is noticeable that the first flush of enthusiasm for checking they are unlocked has waned) and the yet more recent spillage over the throat at Paddington, caused by approaching the terminus at excessive speed. But still so much safer and more restful than the motorway and, lulled by the slight acoustic curtain of the air conditioning, it was straight to sleep. The Mark 3 sleepers are eminently comfortable.

Only enthusiasm to note one operating point on arrival at Paddington; the sleepers were at the back instead of the front. The train had been sent from Taunton to Bristol via Westbury and Bath, which latter place it had therefore run through a second time after reversal at Temple Meads. Taxi to the Charing Cross Hotel. Last time the key was for a room with someone already asleep in it, this to one whose door was open because it was too wide to close. In Southern Railway days, or indeed under the much-respected British Transport Hotels, that would never have happened. The remark is non-political but accurate; the vast majority of railway hotels have deteriorated rapidly under private enterprise.

Soon you will be able to turn right
. . . for France. This was the view
for passengers on the 'day' showing
the storage compound for the
Channel Tunnel works at
Folkestone. Daily trainloads of
concrete segments are moved in
from the Isle of Grain. (*Photo Paul
Savage*)

It's a thankless job and BR's cleaners
do not receive the credit they
deserve. At least this class 143
'Pacer' unit at Newcastle is clean,
thanks to John Wright. Fame at last!
(*Photo Robin Trinder*)

Bridgend situated on the Cardiff–
Swansea main line is served by
sixteen high speed trains to and
from London each day. Arriving at
Bridgend is the 11.41 Swansea–
Paddington service. (*Photo Deryck
Lewis*)

BR's results showing a 'record profit' had just been announced, Sir
Robert Reid claiming the railways were a victim of their own success due
to rapidly-rising traffic. Nowhere is this more of a problem than at
Charing Cross with its six platforms handling more passengers and many,
many more passengers than some of the largest provincial stations. As
always during the rush hour, arriving trains were waiting over the Thames
for a departing service to vacate their platform, many being a few minutes
adrift and sometimes two packed trains disgorging their loads onto the
same island together, making it necessary to queue to walk. A thousand
passengers off, a hundred or so on, crews change ends, and often
departure in less than ten minutes of arrival. Now, try getting the
Western to do that! But then the Western would not leave scruffy
handwritten notices to convey important messages to thousands.

Several business appointments well away from the world of railways,
and then to Liverpool Street, the childhood gateway to London being
transformed brick by brick but much of it still recognisably the same as

St James Deeping signalbox is situated on the Peterborough–Spalding line in Lincolnshire. Sid Clare opens the gates following the passage of a train. (*Photo Paul Savage*)

when a score of tank engines with their Westinghouse brakes puffed away and poured yet more soot into a filthy atmosphere. In steam days the load to London in the morning included several hundredweight of spare collars. Every self-respecting businessman carried one so as to start afresh half way through the day. The writer has watched the changing scene from the changing eating place on the bridge for over half a century. It is all much more civilised, less frantic, less colourful and yet no less chaotic today. David & Charles Publishers was started to prevent having to commute through somewhere like this, less subject to fog and filth but more to technical and labour-relation breakdowns. And what a miserable exit from the capital compared to that out of Paddington; every twist, every arch carries boyhood memories of overtaking or being overtaken by the famous expresses of yesteryear, the range of through services (especially to coastal points) having been curtailed more seriously here than perhaps from any other major terminus. A nostalgic glance at the LNER's summer 1937 timetable showed just how much has been lost; but that is for *LNER 150*.

The location is Par in Cornwall and the time is 14.55. BR Railfreight's class 50 locomotive, *Defiance*, the only one of its class to carry the Railfreight livery, propels its train slowly backwards through the station to enable it to clear the points, after which it will proceed down the Newquay branch. The freight traffic in this part of Britain is predominantly china clay most of which is taken to nearby Fowey Docks for export, although some china clay and slurry is taken to the Midlands for porcelain production and to the Continent. (*Photo Paul Savage*)

Guard Syd Read activates the crossing lights at Stoke Bridge crossing at Ipswich to permit a shunting locomotive to cross in safety – or to put it another way, to protect the road users from 50 tons of locomotive. (*Photo John Day*)

With the lights at red, the shunting locomotive, one of BR's numerous class 08 machines, No 08460, ambles across the road between Ipswich Docks and Ipswich Lower Yard at Stoke Bridge Crossing. (*Photo John Day*)

Heaton depot, at Newcastle, is the maintenance depot for HSTs and multiple units used on the local services. Alan Gilby is fitting a fuel pump to a class 143 'Pacer' unit. (*Photo Robin Trinder*)

It was a colleague's suggestion that a couple of spare hours might be devoted to the North London line, alas not visited during its Broad Street days. So off at Stratford, where you still get something of the feel of it having been a great railway mecca and wonder for what enormous sum BR might eventually sell off hundreds of acres if Dockland's prosperity spreads inland. The booking office handwrote tickets return to North Woolwich and single to Richmond (Liverpool Street reacted as though Richmond were on a different planet and would only issue a ticket to Stratford), and so aboard a particularly derelict two-car EMU, many of its seats not just in bad repair but totally missing. Two young enthusiasts up from Edinburgh for the day were checking the route with the railway atlas and planned to cover the Docklands Light Railway and tube to Woodford – memories of going there by steam made one feel venerable – before returning home for supper.

In Great Eastern days a variety of services terminated at North Woolwich. Now the North London Link, as it is marketed, runs a 20-minute-interval service all the way from Richmond. One has almost come to expect it; no sign of freight, though once it was on a prodigious scale, and the final section down to single track, one engine in steam principle, only one platform, at what was once a dignified terminus, being retained by BR. But, surprise, though it really should not be since it too is happening all over, preservation activity on the adjoining track was evident – noisily so. Beside an ex-Great Eastern coach with its second-class compartments (maybe one used in childhood since parents thought first and third into Liverpool Street equally impossible), a tank engine in fading Kent & East Sussex livery was trying to move another tank but failing with constant slipping. An elderly gentleman was throwing sand by the handful from the platform hoping to hit the rail with a bit to help the engine getting a footing.

'Why don't you use a bucket?' shouted out the EMU driver.

'Because we don't have a bucket,' came the reply.

'So you want to change jobs?' asked the steam driver.

'You'd never make it to Richmond.'

And indeed Richmond seemed light years away, if only 27 stations by the North London Link. As regular as clockwork, every ten minutes a train bound from Richmond to North Woolwich passed in the opposite direction, but not a single freight despite sections of the third-rail electrified route also having overhead electrification for through-freight

working. The only non-North Woolwich train passed was shortly before Richmond on another dual-electrified section, this time London Transport.

People of all kinds. Most were on board only for a station or two, making a strictly local journey or using the line to change somewhere (first of course at Stratford) for London. It began Cockney style and steadily went upmarket. 'G. Davis is innocent,' still declared several graffiti; one woman earnestly read an application form for a UK passport; at Brondesbury Park an enjoyable rural interlude with birdsong; they were found mowing grass the old-fashioned way at West Hampstead; station architecture of course constantly changed, several stations such as Highbury & Ilsington having spacious platforms and buildings, though everywhere facilities still provided for the public were minimal and most buildings kept locked; and traffic held up at the level crossing as the train drifted into Acton Central.

From the railway point of view the North London is a bit like an aerial view of the capital as it crosses the main arteries going east, north and then west. An HST was spotted just having left King's Cross, a brief glimpse

The introduction of the 'Thameslink' trains which provide a north-south service across the capital has been a considerable asset and improvement to London rail travellers. Class 319 units are used on these services and are dual voltage – 750 volt third rail (for use on the Southern Region) and 25kV overhead (for use on the London Midland Region). Unit No 319045 is seen at Bromley South forming the 15.57 Orpington–Bedford service. (*Photo Paul Savage*)

The wagons used on BR's 'merry-go-round' system whereby coal is loaded at a colliery and is discharged automatically at a power station and thence to the colliery again are known as type HAA, and these often have to receive medication on account of the arduous conditions under which they operate. Here, a re-inforcing stanchion is welded into place at Barry Carriage & Wagon Maintenance depot by welder Brian Alcock. HAA wagons in this area are used to ferry coal between the valley collieries and Aberthaw power station. (*Photo Deryck Lewis*)

of the Midland, expresses seen into and out of Euston while waiting at Willesden Junction High Level (a few peak-hour trains from Harrow & Wealdstone or even Watford Junction join the North London here and mainly make their way into Liverpool Street), but the Great Way West was deserted. Once, there was almost always a freight waiting to join the GW on the ramp down from the North London; rarely today. And so through Kew Gardens into Richmond, North Woolwich and dockland stations such as the recently-renamed Silverton & City Airport now in turn seeming in a quite different culture.

The Southern gave a smooth, silent journey in a well-filled obviously sparklingly new EMU through Clapham Junction and around the curves to Waterloo, spacious, gentle, quiet before the start of the daily exodus from London. Not quite the same intensity per platform here as at Charing Cross, but a passenger was saying how he was held up for half an hour in a queue of trains waiting for platforms because two guards had not turned up. The unthinkable is now everyday, Waterloo often a management and personnel nightmare. But there is still space and character, and no doubt this is the sensible place for the London end of

It is 10.40 and all is well at
Newcastle Central, one of many
listed stations due to its architectural
facets. Note the new 'Terrazzo'
flooring which has been applied at
many InterCity stations throughout
Britain. (*Photo Robin Trinder*)

Efficient suspension to give a smooth ride is as important for freight as it is for passengers, preventing wear and damage to stock and track. At Barry Carriage & Wagon Maintenance depot, suspension springs on a HAA wagon are changed by Ken Williams, Colin Fifield, Leighton Jones and Ken Kitcatt, not a job for the fainthearted! There are 14,000 HAA wagons in use throughout the country. (*Photo Deryck Lewis*)

InterCity have introduced Pullman lounges at selected main line stations where travellers with first class tickets and American Express credit cards may wait for their train in luxury surroundings with creature comforts. Two of the latter are pictured here, Louise Nicholls (left) and Pam Clayton. These two young ladies look after the Newcastle Pullman lounge. See you there! (*Photo Robin Trinder*)

the Channel Tunnel services, though heaven forbid that everyone will be expected to clear customs here, throwing away much of the Chunnel's advantage by making through services between the Continent and the North and Scotland impossible.

Like Liverpool Street, Waterloo is not just a station but a series of separate stations or villages happening to be together, the Windsor Line platforms being especially village-like, though most to be disturbed because of the Chunnel. With occasional clockwork-like comings and goings, it seemed more like a provincial station, while the derelict Waterloo & City rolling stock, hard against the buffers of one of the short sidings near the lift down to The Drain, almost conveyed a touch of the preservation site.

At Harwich Parkeston Quay, the shunter couples the locomotive to the stock of the 18.45 service to Liverpool Street. This is the Boat Train and is entitled The Admiral du Ruyter. The shunter is connecting the jumper cables which provide power for the lighting circuits. (*Photo John Day*)

Tyne Yard is an important staging yard for Speedlink trains where wagons are sorted onto differing services. This train is the daily Tees Yard to Craiginches (Aberdeen) service and is pulling out of the vastly reduced (from its original size) Tyne Yard behind class 47 No 47600. (*Photo Neville E. Stead*)

The well-ordered electric silence was broken noisily as class 50 *Renown*, No 50029, came in with an empty rake of coaches for Exeter St David's, No 33106 to become the train engine trailing. They stopped where not only the Atlantic Coast Express but Cunard and P&O specials, many Royal trains and Winston Churchill's steam-hauled funeral train also parked. Much of Waterloo is everyday, almost homely, but there is style, the concourse possibly BR's most successful inheritance from the Southern. And, at least until Chunnel passengers start arriving, there are usually taxis; this one to Euston, the fifth London terminus to be visited within a few hours.

'Are you travelling first class?' asked the receptionist through the intercom at the Pullman lounge. But, when in, one still has to present 'the card' – Pullman or American Express. Many passengers, nearly all for the 16.00 Manchester Pullman, were surprised, and those without American Express mainly found themselves 'not bothered' meaning they disappeared rather than pay BR for its Pullman card, only worthwhile for really regular first-class journeys.

'Tea or coffee?' answered, 'Really weak black tea', brought the usual buffet car response of that it was premixed, though here it is superior, Rombouts. Nothing else free, apart from the newspapers and easy chairs and a couple of useful desks, but still some similarity to an airline first-class lounge. Though the receptionist said she would call passengers, most preferred to make their way to the train earlier, by way of the Superloo; no charge for Pullman lounge passengers, so there was a saving.

Boarding the Manchester Pullman was almost as bad as getting on a 747, a long, slow-moving queue down the ramp beside two other equally slow-moving queues for other trains. Of all the termini visited, only Paddington is yet an open station, the lack of ticket inspection – and particularly of ticket inspectors who start their job a few minutes later than the train is ready and passengers are more than ready – adding a civilising touch under Brunel's great roof. Euston seems no more civilised architecturally or any other way than the day it opened, only beaten by one of the chief destinations it serves – Birmingham New Street – in general undesirability.

The Pullman was welcoming. The trip taken when only the Manchester Pullman survived and the individual, luxury treatment of passengers was out of vogue in the make-everything-standard-and-interchangeable mode, had been a great disappointment; sullen, minimal service, worse and especially dirtier than on the West Country's Golden Hind, then enjoying Gold Star restaurant car service. When it became clear that the Golden Hind would become an HST and that the original concept of separate restaurant and buffet vehicles would have to be abandoned because of declining restaurant car receipts, the service was 'standardised' and West Country businessmen lost options like porridge, potatoes and mushrooms for breakfast. Now the Golden Hind is better than anything the GWR ever provided, excellent in theory and usually made excellent in practice by keen Plymouth-based staff – though whether BR will eventually benefit or suffer from providing full meals only to first-class passengers only time will tell. Certainly those not able to afford first class but who used to enjoy a full breakfast are angry and deprived and would easily be wooed away from the railway if it did not have something of a monopoly in speed and reliability.

Not quite the same devotion among the Manchester Pullman staff, and a fairly abrupt apology; kitchen fault so no hot food, only afternoon tea. This was served from several trollies; adequate rather than luxurious, those in the last of the four-and-a-half 'Pullman cars' – in fact Mark 3 first like any other – kept waiting for special requests like extra hot water. But this Friday a full passenger complement, most alighting well before Manchester, reached quicker by the second evening Pullman an hour later. A smooth, punctual ride, with a chance to enjoy that once commonplace happening even in, say the Welsh Valleys, which is now a rarity anywhere; overtaking a freight (a Freightliner) before our Watford Junction stop, where it overtook us, we to gain the ascendancy a few miles later, demonstrating how speed at a ton or over does eat up the miles.

The clock at Cambridge says one minute to midnight and another day is over – except for BR it is not, for life goes on around the clock. A class 312 unit forms the last arrival of the day with the 22.35 service from Liverpool Street. (*Photo Gordon Bird*)

Private catering now takes place on numerous services around the country. At-your-seat service at 20.10 hrs – can't be bad! This was the scene aboard a class 156 Sprinter working the 15.35 Liverpool–Lowestoft service pictured between Ely and Thetford. (*Photo Gordon Bird*)

Dinner at the Midland Hotel, Manchester, one of the British Transport Hotel's gems which has also been well served by privatisation thanks to Manchester's ratepayers. And back to Piccadilly, formerly London Road, first reached many years ago from Sheffield and the Great Central route, still an extremely busy station but after ten o'clock notably lacking the newspaper traffic that for a century was greater here than anywhere in England outside London. BR without newspaper trains . . . cattle trains, milk trains, and so on and so on. This day's journeying emphasised afresh how much today's railway belies what schoolboys were taught, that passengers were unimportant compared to freight on all railways, at least north of the Thames.

The 22.18 Holidaymaker Express advertised itself as for Macclesfield, Stafford, Wolverhampton, Birmingham New Street, Cheltenham Spa, Bristol Temple Meads, Plymouth, Truro, Hayle, St Erth and Penzance, nine coaches including a buffet. Ian O'Connell, transferred by Travellers Fare to Manchester when made redundant in Liverpool, accidentally put out of a job earlier in the week by the roster clerk assuming he was on holiday, was pleased to have 'the hours' to make up. And hours they were; more or less non-stop duty Manchester to Penzance and back, something BR would have dismissed as uneconomic a few years ago when no catering was provided on trains west of Plymouth, for example. Guard Fazal Ellahi promised a keen driver, and amazingly he came on the inter-com, 'Good evening ladies and gents. This is the driver speaking. May I personally welcome you aboard and I hope you have a pleasant journey and a happy holiday. I'll be taking you to Birmingham where there is a locomotive change.'

He walked through the train, 'Strap yourself in and be ready for the blast off . . . you like a bit of G force, don't you.' It got everybody in the holiday mood, everybody being just over a hundred passengers (about twice that beyond Birmingham), mainly families who had assumed there would be no overnight refreshments and had brought their own festive rations.

A fuel pump goes into the cleaning tank at Heaton depot prior to Dave McCartney undertaking a modification which will improve the pump's performance. (*Photo Robin Trinder*)

Memories of Friday overnight holiday trains of yesteryear came rushing back; packed, slow, usually late – sometimes so late that Saturday morning's return services started back to the Midlands and North hours behind schedule – they were so undesirable as to have encouraged instant car purchase. Many were composed of out-of-date, minimally-maintained rolling stock retained solely to cope with the peak holiday traffic a maximum of a dozen weekends a year, the conveyance of people starting and ending their annual fortnight by the sea being conducted like a military operation, and there never being any question of turning surplus business away because it might be uneconomic. Extra resources were committed to the peak business annually until it reached its inglorious zenith in 1958. The railway's share had been declining for several years by then, but the growth of tourism was so great that in absolute numbers more continued to travel by train – 30,000 on the busiest Saturdays down the Torbay line from destinations beyond Bristol, for example.

The new train ferry, *Nord Pas de Calais*, introduced in 1988 gently manoeuvres into the dock at Dover. The rail wagons can be seen awaiting unloading. This ferry is now the only rail ferry linking Britain with Europe, the rail ferry service from Parkeston Quay to Zeebrugge having ceased operation in 1986. (*Photo Paul Savage*)

Three class 33 locomotives have been nominated to shunt the ferry traffic on and off the train ferry. This picture shows two of these locomotives at work, Nos 33302 and 33206 both drawing forward with vehicles full of produce. Never mind the balance of payments! (*Photo Paul Savage*)

It would have been with a heavy heart one would have joined the Friday night 'express' from Manchester to Penzance thirty years ago. Well over twelve hours were consumed in usually pretty awful conditions, certainly without any refreshment service (and at times trains were so crowded you could not have made your way along the corridor anyway) even if the thing ran to time. 'As usual the overnight trains from the Midlands and North arrived in the West Country between one and two hours late, many of them in the wrong order making operating conditions difficult,' was a typical Press comment. West Country newspapers commented on the weekend changeover as though it were a sporting event.

But tonight a Mark 3, not surprisingly the only first-class passenger in the only first-class coach not marked down for bargain use – and only a couple of takers at £3 a head for that. An exhilarating run, perfect timing. Into Bristol early in just 3½ hours, making the overall time scheduled from Manchester to Penzance in one minute shy of nine hours seem very comfortable. That includes over half-an-hour in Temple Meads, a recovery period allowed all overnight trains and which would no doubt have been useful for the following Newcastle–Newquay HST shown as running 20 minutes late. If it did not get onto the Newquay branch, which now ends at a single-track buffer stop at an unstaffed station, all six summer Saturday services being HSTs, there would be trouble. A trip on the inaugural Paddington Atlantic Coast Express to Newquay complete with full restaurant car had gone splendidly a few weeks before, though just as BR cashes in on the leisure business afresh with such initiatives as this and the tourist Pullmans making good use of business sets during the centre-of-the-day lull, it was terrifying to hear the Transport Minister, David Mitchell, declare, 'British Rail is not in the leisure business', as justification for selling off the Settle & Carlisle. But this very day's takings were swollen by charters decidedly in the leisure business such as an intriguing Pullman charter from Llandovery to Machynlleth, the VSOE Welsh Land Cruise. And were not BR benefiting from ten trains all booked full celebrating the fiftieth birthday of *Mallard* achieving the still-unbroken steam speed record?

Five long-distance trains were taking their nocturnal sojourn at Temple Meads together, including an HST from the West to Manchester with less than a dozen passengers aboard, and the up-sleeper patronised just 24 hours before. It was getting to be a long day! One knew the sleeper was in from the presence of a woman attendant (who during GWR 150 refused to allow passengers to alight at Paddington until they had expressed appreciation for BR allowing a DMU to be painted in chocolate and cream) waiting for a male colleague to emerge from the toilet. Up and down sleepers are eventually side-by-side allowing gossip between their staffs a little earlier as are the two Great Western TPOs (and they are genuinely still called Great Western as you will see from the postmark if you pop a late letter to yourself through the slot of one of the sorting vehicles) where a total of over 300 Post Office staff are at work on the station for a furious half hour (or at least they were when this was written). The time-honoured pattern has since been radically changed, several new TPOs now running, Paddington–Penzance going via the Berks & Hants, there being a separate Paddington–Swansea; and York–Bristol is now extended to Plymouth – a jump in activity when with the demise of newspaper trains and increasing use of air by the Post Office, many felt the days of TPOs were numbered.

The buffet on platform 3 is open especially for passengers, the station announcer repeated as each train arrived. But for this passenger it was into the very same berth as used on the up-journey the previous evening for a quick snooze before Newton Abbot.

There are many worse ways of spending a day. Glorious scenery, ever-changing cultural backgrounds and dialects and, of course, the railway interest. Apart from the start from Newton Abbot, everything had run to time. It was not cheap, but then genuine business had been transacted in London and Manchester, and much paperwork done en route, especially to and from Manchester. Incidentally, superb though the riding of the HSTs is from most points of view, writing is much easier on locomotive-hauled trains, even at high speed on West Coast main line track in places distinctly the worse for wear. The HSTs have more up-and-down movement, never great, constantly corrected, but enough to make it hard to keep your pen on the paper. But then the trip on the Manchester Pullman as on any Golden Hind or other business train demonstrated that pen and paper are becoming outmoded. Over half the passengers were using a telephone, dictating machine or personal computer, or all three.

What one did hear during the day were numerous complaints about BR as well as occasional praises. Staff who were rude, offices which ignored correspondence even when the enquiry was for 300 long-distance bookings, rules unimaginatively applied or plain invented to be obstructive, fare structures that even the staff did not understand . . . the mutterings go on ceaselessly even when passengers feel they get reasonable value for most journeys. The engine driver of the Holiday-maker Express out of Manchester had shown what a touch of personality can do to make people smile.

The system survives, loses less money, generally works better, and the public by and large think it gives reasonable value. This traveller could not expect to be provided better by private enterprise and the lack of a unified system would hurt, yet if BR does go down it will surely be because it did not get its management act together soon enough, has still not conquered the problem of staff morale, and too frequently allows the customer to feel that he is not special or even wanted.

Newton Abbot is, without doubt, a 'Resort for Railfans', for the station witnesses a large variety of traffic throughout the 24 hours. There is a constant procession of InterCity High Speed Trains en route to and from London and the north east, as well as a declining number of locomotive hauled express services. Railfreight traffic figures prominently, whilst Provincial Services sector trains are evident, with the local services including those to Paignton. The West of England Travelling Post Office (TPO) also has Newton Abbot on its list of stops. This picture shows InterCity doing good business with, on the left, a London-bound High Speed Train from Plymouth whilst adjacent is a class 47 locomotive-hauled express waiting to depart for Plymouth. The site of the Newton Abbot diesel depot can be seen on the right. (*Photo Geoffrey Kichenside*)

NEWTON ABBOT SNAPSHOT

Of all the stations in the West Country, Newton Abbot, in July 1988, seemed but a pale shadow of its former self, even two years before. Where there had once been a major junction station with six through-running lines, extensive carriage sidings, an important locomotive depot and workshops and a marshalling yard, a forest of semaphore signals controlled from two of the largest mechanical signalboxes on the old Great Western system, there were now but three through lines, colour-light signals controlled from the new distant Exeter signalling centre with electronic and computer gadgetry and nothing much else. True the two island platforms with extensive gabled roofs were still there – at least they had not been sacrificed to bus-stop shelters seen in other parts of the country – and so was the major station entrance building and office complex dating from the 1920s, although with the offices on the middle and upper floors no longer housing the railway staff for whom they were built. Everything else, though, had virtually gone, the old engine shed building still just there but very derelict, and weed-grown open space where sidings had once lain. What had been the up main platform No 4 on the town side was now part of the much enlarged car park opened with due ceremony a year earlier by BR's InterCity Director, Dr John Prideaux, for whom to an extent it was a homecoming since he had been the area manager at Newton Abbot in the mid 1970s. By July 1988 Newton Abbot no longer had its own management and was controlled by Exeter. The removal of the track at platform 4 and the adjoining up through line, used until the end by non-stopping trains including the Cornish Riviera Express, has meant that the platform on the town side of the station was no longer physically isolated other than by the footbridge from the station entrance building, and ramps now link the booking hall directly with platform 3, used by most trains towards London and the North. Moreover, Newton Abbot is now an open station so that there are no ticket barriers, and passengers arriving by car with pre-booked tickets can walk straight on to platform 3 from the car park.

Work was still in hand putting the finishing touches to the new ramp from the booking hall to the platform on 'our day' with a gang of bricklayers working on the access doorway. But they were not the only working team at Newton Abbot that day. The entrance building as a whole was undergoing renovation and was surrounded by scaffolding clad in green netting to stop wayward pieces of brick and concrete from falling widely below as the corroded 1920s' steel window frames in the upper floors were

Coal is also exported from Blyth and there is much daily activity in this forgotten part of England, rarely visited except by railway photographers! Two class 08 shunters illustrate the chores that are the lifeblood of the rail business in Northumberland – No 08886 propels loaded coal wagons at the top of the picture onto the staithes where coal will be discharged into the ships, whilst sister No 08421 draws empties preparatory to being taken to collieries for loading. (*Photo Neville E. Stead*)

One of BR's construction projects is a new rail link to Stansted airport. It involves the provision of a new track – and a tunnel – from the main Liverpool Street–Cambridge line near Bishops Stortford. These two pictures show the work in progress on the chosen day. The train passing is the 11.00 King's Lynn Liverpool Street service headed by a class 86 locomotive. When the new branch has been completed, it will be served by brand new class 322 units, similar to the existing class 321 Anglia Electric, but with increased luggage accommodation. (*Photos Gordon Bird*)

renewed. Under the platform canopies another gang was installing new lighting units.

From an operating viewpoint the most startling change was the increase in speed permitted to non-stopping trains, which, with considerable slewing of the surviving tracks, has allowed the easing of the curves at each end of the station. No longer do trains have to slow to 35mph but can pass through at 60mph. Moreover, all three tracks are reversible, which allows trains to appear from unexpected directions. Certainly the new layout provides the bare minimum of facilities but does allow flexibility if the signalmen at Exeter are prepared to be flexible and change

booked platforms, especially where conflict can occur on the flat junction – in reality a series of simple crossovers – between the Paignton branch and the Plymouth main line. This was adequately demonstrated on this day during a mid-morning rush when six trains were handled at Newton Abbot in the space of thirty minutes, four of them passenger trains, all late, only by a few minutes but none exactly to time, although one arrived on time but was delayed by a late-running train off the Paignton line in front of it, this being a case where the flexible layout was not used to save delay.

First of the group was the 07.40 Paddington to Plymouth, booked to call at Newton Abbot at 10.40/1. Shown in the timetable just as an InterCity train rather than an InterCity 125, second class ticket holders could have hardly expected the luxury of first class accommodation yet eight of the ten Mk 2 coaches were first class, seven of them labelled for the use of second class passengers. Headed by locomotive No 47477 it arrived one minute late but overstayed its calling time and left four minutes late. Hard on its heels, and indeed running on single yellows through the station while the 07.40 from Paddington was little further than the former Aller Junction, came three class 50s coupled together,

107

50 004/16/46, undoubtedly bound for Laira depot, for the latter had a most enormous flat on one wheel set, the thump of which shook the station foundations as it passed.

The next train should have been an up service, the 10.35 Paignton–Paddington due to call at platform 3 from 10.50 to 10.52 but shown on the departure television monitor as running 11 minutes late and in reverse order with the first class at the Paignton end. But at 11.01 rather than the up-Paignton service it was the 08.10 Paddington–Penzance train which drew to a stand at platform 2 right on time. Although leaving London only half-an-hour after the 07.40, the 08.10 had travelled via Swindon, Bath and Bristol yet, despite the extra mileage, its higher speed and fewer stops meant that it was closing up on the 07.40 and by Plymouth should have been only 14 minutes behind. However, today the signal at the Plymouth end of platform 2 remained at red for another four minutes while the late-running 10.35 from Paignton snaked its way over the crossovers across the path of the Penzance train instead of running up the branch track to platform 1. At 11.05 the signal cleared to green for the 08.10 from Paddington, which left immediately, passing the 10.35 from Paignton under the bridge carrying the Torquay road over the railway. When the 10.35 arrived it was, in fact, a North East–South West InterCity 125 set with just one first class coach, having been substituted for the usual London set. It was away at 11.09, now 19 minutes late, just as a down freight passed on platform 2 line, slowing as its driver saw the single yellow in the platform end signal as the 08.10 from Paddington tackled the climb towards Dainton summit. The freight, headed by 47201, was a lengthy affair of 21 wagons, including English China Clay's bogie clay wagons, BP liquid petroleum gas tanks, Railfreight vans and some train ferry cargo wagons and tank cars hopefully

'Can you hear me, mother?' Communication is the name of the game with signalmen. The Thetford signalman gets on the blower to a colleague down the line. (*Photo Gordon Bird*)

The driver of the 16.35 Liverpool Street–King's Lynn, The Fenman, looks back to the platform at Magdalen Road, waiting for the right away. Network SouthEast Anglia sub-sector operates the 96 miles between London and King's Lynn using electric traction between Liverpool Street and Cambridge and class 47 diesels between Cambridge and Lynn. (*Photo Gordon Bird*)

'Damn! They've forgotten me'. King's Lynn station entrance at 18.00 and a traveller waits for inspiration or a lift. (*Photo Gordon Bird*)

The time? 05.30 and another day starts for the newsagent on March station as he prepares the papers for the morning rush. March has always been a mecca for railway enthusiasts and the range of books reflects this fact. However, March as a railway centre has been declining in recent years – the 'Joint' line to Spalding was closed, one of the marshalling yards followed suit and the diesel depot is now a shadow of its former self. (*Photo Gordon Bird*)

foreshadowing an expansion of through rail freight with the opening of the Channel Tunnel in five years time.

The modest delays continued for one more train, the 10.48 Paignton–Cardiff, due to call at 11.05/6 but already delayed by the preceding 10.35 from Paignton and by the down freight. It was shown as on time on the departure screen but actually arrived at 11.12, a two-car Sprinter No 155 328. In other respects the television information displays were remarkably informative: 'Super Sprinters have passenger buttons to open doors'. All very fine as long as the passengers know the detail differences between Sprinters and Super Sprinters, or Super Sprinters and InterCity 125s, or Pacers, or Skippers, or plain old fashioned railway carriages with or without air conditioning. Most passengers would not have a clue and certainly many have found that the button in the Sprinters, which looks as though it is to open the toilet door, in fact operates the emergency brakes and alarm signal much to their embarrassment.

Heaton depot, Newcastle, is one of four depots which look after the HSTs that operate the East Coast main line services, the other three being Bounds Green, London, Neville Hill, Leeds, and Craigentinny, Edinburgh. Ken Purdy, Production Manager at Heaton, inspects a bogie on a power car. (*Photo Robin Trinder*)

King's Lynn docks have seen a revival in recent years and rail has benefited from the transport of imported goods. There was little activity taking place at 17.50 when this picture was taken, but evidence of some of the traffic – imported coal – can be seen on the dockside as loaded HAA wagons await movement. (*Photo Gordon Bird*)

By the evening, most trains were running to time but two trains from the North were very late. Between 19.00 and 20.30, fifteen trains called at or passed Newton Abbot, but four were empty trains. Of the rest, most performed as booked. The Paignton line by that time was being served by a branch train which had run through from Exmouth calling at 18.52 to 19.03, returning by 19.41 and leaving again at 19.50, coming back a second time at 20.20 – this time empty – and leaving for Paignton at 20.25. Unusually this working was formed of two single diesel cars, 55000/26. But then since the Skipper debacle in the West Country – did no-one in high places on BR really consider what the effects would be on long wheelbase lightweight four-wheel railcars on some of the steeply-graded, sharply-curved lines in the South West? – which resulted in these totally unsuitable trains being moved up country within a couple of years of being built, the replacements have included many of the first generation diesel multiple-unit survivors, now 25 and more years old from

'Can I have a return ticket, please?'
'Yes, sir, where to?' 'Back here, of
course'. Newcastle Central station
booking office and Lynn Whale
issues an advance ticket. (*Photo
Robin Trinder*)

The Northumberland coal field is
big business for British Rail and its
depot at Cambois, Blyth, services
class 56 locomotives which operate
the numerous coal trains from the
collieries to power stations. Most of
the coal is forwarded to Blyth power
station, although some coal is sent
by rail to the Aire Valley power
stations. This train is conveying
empty merry-go-round wagons back
to Tynemouth from Blyth, headed
by class 56 No 56119. (*Photo Neville
E. Stead*)

March station at 05.50 and
passengers are awaiting the arrival of
the 05.49 service to Birmingham
from Norwich and the service to
Blackpool (05.13 from Cambridge).
On the opposite platform, the 05.32
from Peterborough arrives en route
to Cambridge. (*Photo Gordon Bird*)

other parts of the country to supplement the suburban pattern DMUs with side doors to each bay of seats favoured by the WR.

InterCity 125 sets predominated on the long distance evening services, although the 13.25 Liverpool Lime Street to Plymouth headed by locomotive No 47621 was a remarkably short formation of full brake, buffet car, two open seconds, a corridor brake first and another open second. It was nevertheless right to time. The following North East–South West service, the 13.10 Newcastle–Plymouth was not so lucky but was gaining time south of Birmingham to judge by the reducing delay shown on the television screen. It was due at 19.45 but at 19.15 was shown as 48 minutes late; a few minutes later the delay had come down to 30 minutes, presumably as it had entered the Exeter control area approaching Taunton. But it lost whatever path it had for it was now behind the Golden Hind Pullman, which was right on time into Newton Abbot at 20.11. Perhaps the ambience of the first class InterCity 125 cars designated as Pullman was improved by the red roses on the tables and the quality dinner just coming to an end. The evening peak at Newton Abbot was now in full swing as this commuter train arrived from London, for at platform 3 came the 17.30 Penzance–Cardiff, a two-car Super Sprinter with Trailfare catering trolley. The Golden Hind Pullman headed west and the Super Sprinter east, passing the late running Newcastle train running just five minutes behind the Pullman. Hopefully the Golden Hind would be held at Plymouth for any passengers off the Newcastle train wanting a connection on towards Penzance. As for the Devon Scot, the 08.45 Aberdeen–Plymouth due at Newton Abbot at 20.32, the television screen told a familiar depressing story – 31 minutes late at 19.15 (when it was leaving Bristol) and by 20.20 it was 40 minutes late.

Just one day in the life of British Rail. It was not perfect. Nor was the day before, or the day after. But it showed that timekeeping is an area which needs much attention from the top through to the men in the signalboxes and in driving cabs, if BR is to be a competitive force in the 1990s.

At Westerfield, the driver of the 07.14 Lowestoft–Ipswich service can be seen using the radio telephone to inform the signalman at Saxmundham that he has arrived at Westerfield. Control will then be handed over to the Colchester power box for the remainder of the journey to Ipswich. (*Photo John Day*)

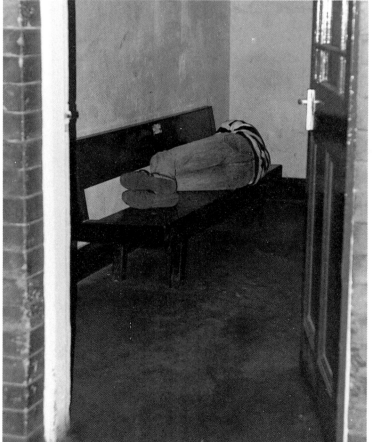

As a church clock finishes striking midnight at Warrington Bank Quay, a young man bereft of either top coat or luggage bunks down in the southbound waiting room, oblivious to the arrival and departure of the first two trains outside. (*Photo Eddie Bellass*)

Saxmundham is the radio signalling centre which controls the East Suffolk line from Ipswich to Lowestoft. The actual section controlled by radio is from Westerfield to Ipswich. This was BR's first route to be converted to radio signalling (Radio Electronic Token Block, to give it its correct nomenclature). BR spent £1.25m investing in this equipment which has safeguarded the route's future by dramatically reducing operating costs. Entering the station is the 07.10 Ipswich–Lowestoft formed of a 3-car class 101 set. These multiple units are based at Norwich depot for maintenance purposes. (*Photo John Day*)

Amidst life, there is death . . . At Snailwell, a small village near Newmarket in Suffolk, is the site of Mayer Newman Ltd, one of only three scrap processors who dispose of BR's blue asbestos-contaminated rolling stock. Coaches and multiple units containing this dangerous insulating material are put through a firing tunnel which burns the interiors and so exposes the asbestos. This is swilled off after the gas burners have been extinguished and the slurry is deposited into tanks which are emptied every week and despatched to a controlled tip. These pictures show a Cravens multiple unit coach having been dragged out of the tunnel after firing. Note the heat has bent the underframe. The residual metal, now devoid of asbestos, will be quickly fragmentised and sorted according to type of metal. Meanwhile, the asbestos slurry is seen being deposited into the tanks ready for disposal by road to a Cambridgeshire tip. (*Photos Gordon Bird*)

An evening Speedlink freight from Mossend prepares to descend into Arpley yard in charge of 86415 and 85018. The time is 00.08. (*Photo Eddie Bellass*)

The time – 00.03; the location – Warrington. The 00.01 (MX) parcels train, barred to passengers since early 1987, is already 3 minutes late for its date with the Holyhead mail at Chester. (*Photo Eddie Bellass*)

Six minutes past midnight at Warrington; although sleeping car passengers can now bed down all the way to London, those in seating accommodation on the 22.00 Barrow–Euston have just another 52 minutes to go before being turned out to change at Stafford. (*Photo Eddie Bellass*)

Sister locomotive to 37901, No 37902, one of the six locomotives of this sub-class allocated to steel traffic duties, heads south at St Devereux near Pontrilas on the North & West route with steel empties from Dee Marsh (Shotton steelworks) to Margam. (*Photo John C. Baker*)

24 hrs WITH CLASS 37 No 37901

British Rail's locomotive fleet is now sectorised; this means that all locomotives are specifically allocated to pools which are used to provide traction for the sub-sectors of the railway business. Thus, for instance, class 86 electric locomotive No 86503 is allocated to the Freightliners pool and is thus used for this specific purpose of hauling Freightliners. Locomotives must not be used for other traffic unless prior permission has been obtained from the requisite 'owner'.

The allocation of locomotives to pools has had a dramatic effect. The first has been a reduction in the number of locomotives needed, as far greater efficiency is derived and secondly, reliability has been improved due to the maintenance staff now taking a greater interest in 'their' locomotives, which are always returned to the respective depots instead of the previous practice where locomotives could, and did, stray all over the country, being used for any type of train.

This feature focusses on class 37 No 37901. It is one of six locomotives based at Cardiff Canton depot and which are totally dedicated for use with the steel traffic. Nos 37901-6 are different from their sisters – they have been re-engined, four (including 37901) with GEC power units and two with Mirrlees power units. These six machines have already amassed a good record of reliability since being re-engined.

There are various rosters (or diagrams, to give the correct terminology) for these locomotives and the day for 37901 begins at 00.50 in the early hours when the loco moves off Canton depot at Cardiff and heads for Tidal Sidings Yard, Cardiff, which takes it 25 minutes to reach.

There it attaches itself to train 6M44 which is the 01.45 Tidal Sidings to Dee Marsh. The train calls at Llanwern at 02.32 and leaves at 03.47 loaded with hot rolled coil (HRC). This section of line is a major freight artery and 37901 powers on to Newport where it diverges and heads north on the North & West line which takes the train through Hereford, Craven Arms and on to Shrewsbury. During the journey the train has to surmount one of the country's famous railway inclines – Llanvihangel near Abergavenny and the sound of the GEC power unit in full song will reverberate across the Monmouthshire countryside.

Shrewsbury is reached at 07.01 where a crew change is made, the train leaving immediately at 07.03. It is a climb out of Shrewsbury past Coton Hill and 6M44 proceeds on to Wrexham where it branches off onto the former Great Central Railway's lines and heads for Dee Marsh. The time is now 08.36.

Strictly speaking outside the period of this log; the previous day's Warrington, 22.55 departure to Blackpool appears here due to being 87 min late. (*Photo Eddie Bellass*)

The night supervisor at Warrington Bank Quay logs in a reasonably satisfactory report on southbound services before concerning himself with the northbound situation, with all Inter City trains at least 90 minutes down. (*Photo Eddie Bellass*)

Upon reaching its destination, 37901 propels its train into the sidings and is detached, the wagons being taken into the Shotton steelworks (formerly the John Summers steelworks) by one of the privately owned British Steel diesel shunters.

Meanwhile, it is time for 37901 to proceed on its own (light engine) to Crewe. It is timed to depart at 09.10 and travels back to Shrewsbury where another crew change is made and an hour's stop is taken. Arrival at Crewe's Gresty Lane depot is scheduled at 12.29.

Whilst 37901 has been taking its load of HRC to Dee Marsh and then travelling to Crewe, another loaded steel train has been making its way south from Mossend near Glasgow. It is the 06.35 Mossend–Cardiff Tidal Sidings and 37901's duty is to take over the train at Crewe and haul it on its last leg of the journey.

At 13.18, 37901 moves out of Crewe with the 6V75 train of HRC

destined for finishing at the South Wales steelworks. HRC is finished at both Shotton and at Llanwern. After retracing its steps (or wheels!) to Shrewsbury, it is the North & West route all the way to Newport and thence on to Cardiff. It is now 18.32, but 37901 is far from finished.

A local trip working, the 6B56, is now scheduled, this being the 19.30 Tidal Sidings to Waunllwyd (pronounced Wine-thluid). The train calls in at Pengam sidings en route at 19.45 where the loco runs round its train to proceed in the other direction. Leaving Pengam, 6B56 rolls into Margam at 21.00 and finally departs for Waunllwyd one hour later at 22.00, arriving at its destination at 00.07.

Detaching from its train, 37901 leaves Waunllwyd Yard at 00.15 and travels light engine to Godfrey Road stabling point at Newport where the day's work finally comes to an end.

Because the locomotive does not finish its diagram at Cardiff Canton,

this means that a sister locomotive will work the diagram the following day, whilst 37901 will now work a diagram which commences at Newport.

This typical diagram clearly shows the work which is now extricated from locomotives and the exacting nature of the work, which often necessitates working the engine hard for long periods. The South Wales steel traffic is a valuable commodity for BR and the attention to detail in terms of service to the customer (British Steel) is of a high order. Nos 37901-6 are held in high regard at Canton depot where, as aforementioned, the staff's attention to sound maintenance has resulted in these locomotives giving outstanding service.

TABLE OF DAY'S ROSTER FOR LOCO 37901

	Arr	Dep	Train
Cardiff Canton		00.50	Light Engine
Cardiff Tidal Sidings	01.15	01.45	6M44
Dee Marsh Yard	08.36	09.10	Light Engine
Crewe Gresty Lane	12.29	13.18	6V75
Cardiff Tidal Sidings	18.32	19.30	6B56
Pengam Sidings	19.45	20.05	6B56
Margam	21.00	22.00	6B56
Waunllwyd	00.07	00.15	Light Engine
Godfrey Road, Newport	01.15		

Already half-an-hour into his morning conference, Warrington Area Manager Ron Couchman (centre) peruses a print-out of the previous day's performance figures as his Operations Manager Tom Rotherham (right) consults the area train crew and yard chiefs. (*Photo Eddie Bellass*)

Warrington full loads yard foreman Jerry Walsh meets the Dallam postman who has brought packets of waybills for everything from whisky to wire rope. (*Photo Eddie Bellass*)

This slumbering sorter from Perth was able to enjoy an extra 85 min nap at Warrington due to the 85 min lateness of his return working – the 20.35 Euston–Aberdeen TPO. (*Photo Eddie Bellass*)

08642 kicks a short rake of bulk powder tankers into No 1 road, at Arpley Yard at 09.30. (*Photo Eddie Belass*)

Many stations throughout the country have a station pet. Tiddles at Warrington TOPS office, is persuaded that the tinned supplementaries to his regular own-brand diet of yard rodents are not yet due. (*Photo Eddie Bellass*)

Warrington TOPS Office at 09.55: during a break time for the shunters, 08642's burbling engine blends in with the soft chunk of still-busy computer keys. (*Photo Eddie Bellass*)

Four hours into the 06.00–14.00 shift at Warrington TOPS office, it's still heads down for the office staff as 08924 idles during the driver's own break. (*Photo Eddie Bellass*)

Mid morning at Haydock Oil Terminal. Resembling a river the day before, the mothballed run-round at Haydock Park emerges from a receding flood at a point where thoroughbred racehorse traffic was handled for the first 60 years of this century. (*Photo Eddie Bellass*)

For the 21st year in succession, the stores were right out of firebars for Stanier Black 5 steam locomotives. This office is at Springs Branch depot. (*Photo Eddie Bellass*)

Signalman Joe Kent at Rainford Junction hands the single line token for Kirkby to the driver of an afternoon class 110 DMU from Manchester Victoria. It was his penultimate day as relief signalman there, for he became the regular man from the following Monday! (*Photo Eddie Bellass*)

Just time to buy 20 ciggies at Sandhills, north Liverpool. (*Photo Eddie Bellass*)

A Merseyrail guard looks down the Helsby line at Hooton for signs of a late DMU. (*Photo Eddie Bellass*)

Public debut for a unique locomotive. The day of the review of BR witnesses the first public run in revenue earning service of the Brush designed, BREL Crewe built class 89 locomotive No 89001. This sleek 125mph machine is maintained by Bounds Green depot and its first duty was to work the 17.36 King's Cross–Peterborough commuter special. Thereafter it was scheduled to work the 07.00 from Peterborough and the 17.36 return. The King's Cross shunter gives the class 89 an admiring glance shortly before its maiden run. (*Photo Brian Beer*)

Occasionally, even the degreasing bath needs degreasing, as is happening here at Springs Branch depot. (*Photo Eddie Bellass*)

An oil company diesel shunter brings a train of loaded tankers across the road onto the BR interchange sidings between Ellesmere Port and Stanlow. (*Photo Eddie Bellass*)

Class 142 No 142034 leads No 150124 into Helsby on the 14.47 Bangor–Hull Trans-Pennine service, the Pacer coming off at Manchester Victoria. (*Photo Eddie Bellass*)

BR painters apply the finishing
touches to Portsmouth & Southsea
station following its extensive
modernisation. The train is the
09.22 from Waterloo. Painters come
under the jurisdiction of BR's Civil
Engineering department. (*Photo
Paul Savage*)

Post Office staff at Bristol Temple
Meads are seen at work on the 14.28
parcels train which runs from
Plymouth to Newcastle. Most of this
traffic goes forward on the 19.35
Bristol–Derby postal train. (*Photo
Mike Goodfield*)

The driver of the 21.05 departure to Liverpool operates his train crew door button after changing ends at Ormskirk. The time is 21.04. (*Photo Eddie Bellass*)

The permanent way department has already half-demolished its own yard at St Helens as No 142034 sweeps in en route from Preston to Liverpool Lime Street. (*Photo Eddie Bellass*)

Friday night is disco night in Liverpool, from which this young couple will return at 02.00 in a taxi, thus booking single from Aughton Park. (*Photo Eddie Bellass*)

THE POLITICAL OVERVIEW

British Rail is a big business, both in size and in turnover. It is intensely a human business and one dogged with politics. Because it is a nationalised industry, it is reportable to the government in the form of the Department of Transport, presided over by the Secretary of State for Transport. Nevertheless, BR is permitted to run its own business, but with stringent controls exercised by the Department of Transport.

Since January, 1982, the country's national railway system has been managed with five business managers called sector directors, these being Railfreight, Network SouthEast, InterCity, Parcels and Provincial. This new style of managerial business-led railway, introduced by Sir Bob Reid, has dramatically transformed the operation of the system. The end result (though far from ended, as it is an on-going exercise) is a far more efficient railway operation where every expenditure, including salaries, has to be justified and accounted for.

One inevitability of this change in managerial style has been the realisation that the railway is no longer a service, but a business. Successive Conservative governments have mandated senior railway managers to either drastically reduce the subsidy the individual business requires, or to operate without any subsidy at all. Those businesses which are now free standing and have to cover all costs with no government assistance are: InterCity, Railfreight and Parcels. The two supported sectors, Provincial and Network SouthEast, are seeing vastly reduced subsidies imposed upon them.

British Rail has to find its investment finance from its own resources. Many pro-rail minded people in the country find this baffling – if a railway system is nationalised, surely the government should fund the infrastructure? Public money from taxes is used to fund motorways, but these same taxes are not used to electrify a main line. Even if BR wishes to borrow money from banking sources, it is limited to the amount it can borrow by means of the External Financing Limit.

British Rail tends to prosper when a Conservative government is in

Tidal Yard at Cardiff receives and despatches numerous trains throughout the day. These are predominantly those operated by Railfreight Metals sub-sector conveying products from the various steelworks. Mr T. G. Jones is the Yard Manager on whose shoulders is considerable responsibility for the efficient operation of the yard. All was running well when this picture was taken – and not a cup of tea in sight! (*Photo Michael Rhodes*)

power, though this has not always been so. Dr Beeching was directed to make the railways more lean by a Conservative government in the early 1960s and many lines were closed. The following Labour government, however, did not reverse the process and lines continued to close. Recent interviews with respective party spokespersons have confirmed the traditional party line that Labour believes in supporting the railways with subsidies whilst the Conservatives are committed to reducing, as far as possible, state aid.

Present day government has taken a more positive attitude to Britain's rail system, partly because of Sir Bob Reid's proven capability as an outstanding railwayman and his business-led style in keeping with the government's prevailing policies, and partly because so much of the railway's fleet was literally worn out that there is not much alternative option than to authorise renewals. However, the way BR now conducts itself, and its far more efficient procedures in dealing with investment proposals, result in a far quicker go-ahead from the government for new orders to be placed.

Nevertheless, BR's investment plans have to provide a 7% return on finance invested before the government will authorise any new scheme, be it a resignalling scheme or a new order for multiple units. Whilst this figure of 7% would be considered small by private business concerns, British Rail has to overcome a major problem when submitting investment plans for approval. Many private investment submissions incorporate cost benefit analysis which takes into account many significant external benefits which are not directly accounted for with the submission. For instance, a road scheme will take into account a benefit of a

Waterloo station and the rush is on. This is the way of life for thousands of people. At least these lucky folk have a new train – a class 455 unit which has just arrived from Hampton Court. (*Photo Paul Savage*)

Peterborough Power Box at 21.22. This is one of six which will eventually cover the whole of the East Coast main line from King's Cross to Edinburgh. Peterborough's area of operation extends from Sandy (42 miles from King's Cross) to Stoke, near Grantham (100 miles from King's Cross). The station announcer sits on one of these chairs. 'British Rail regrets there'll be no regrets today'! (*Photo A. Duncan*)

On the left of the luggage office:

Left luggage
office

Open:-
Weekdays
0615-2300
Sundays
0630-2200

On the counter sign:

Explosive
detector
in use
passengers
must be
prepared to
open luggage
for inspection

'I'm looking for a woman . . . on second thoughts, I will settle for a brolly'. Left luggage is big business for British Rail and tales of the astonishing variety of items left annually is legion. They have a few tales to tell at Waterloo Left Luggage office, but brollies reign supreme! (*Photo Paul Savage*)

British Rail pays the total cost of electrification projects with no government help. The Oslo boat train from Liverpool Street to Harwich Town passes Wrabness near journey's end. (*Photo John C. Baker*)

road user being able to travel quicker to a destination, which therefore can be determined in a saving of money. BR is totally denied the same guidelines and rules when preparing investment plans, a source of great frustration to BR managers and pro-rail supporters. It is a salutary thought that if the same rules applied to rail investment plans as are found at present with road investment schemes, BR would have been able to electrify literally hundreds of miles of track and actually re-open freight lines to passenger train operation. The unwillingness to change the rules in favour of making rail and road comparable in investment criteria is one of BR's biggest millstones.

1987 was the year when privatisation reared its inevitable head. As one of the last large industries still carrying the banner of being state owned, it was revealed that various policy bodies were investigating how and when BR could be hived-off to the private sector. Permutations are many,

and these include the idea of a track and signalling body with operators paying to use the infrastructure; a return to the old style companies such as the LNER and GWR, but this time based on the present regional geographical areas. Sir Bob Reid, BR's present chairman, favours the retention of the existing rail business to keep together the unified, centralised and highly integrated present BR network. Opponents argue that competition is vital for the consumer.

Much of BR is already in private hands. Station catering, a third of the freight rolling stock and a small number of locomotives and coaches are now privately operated. Several management buy-outs have taken over large workshops including the former Doncaster Wagon Works and British Rail Engineering Ltd.

Britain's railway system has become a model system in the past five years, so much so that other countries are now taking note of how BR is operated. It is a source of much chagrin that BR receives so little direct investment compared to other European concerns. (The French government, for instance, wrote out the multi-million francs cheque for the new Trains de Grande Vitesse (TGV) and yet Britain's proposed high speed rail link with the Channel Tunnel will have to be financed privately.)

Notwithstanding this arm's length relationship between the government of the day and BR, the future augers well for the foreseeable future. The government has been steadily authorising major renewal plans for signalling, rolling stock, locomotives and electrification schemes and has publicly stated that it has no intention of embarking on a major change to the size of the rail network.

The Isle of Wight services are managed by Network SouthEast and use ex-Underground stock some of which dates from 1923. On the day under review, the 12.07 from Shanklin arrives at Ryde Pier during the unit's last year of service. Newer stock dating from only 1938(!) takes over in 1989. (*Photo Paul Savage*)

All the Isle of Wight vehicles are maintained at Ryde workshops. Coach No 94 is pictured undergoing overhaul with the island's resident diesel shunter, No 03079, in the background. (*Photo Paul Savage*)

An everyday occurrence for thousands of commuters – paying the car park attendant. It was 06.45 when this picture was taken at Peterborough which has seen a huge rise in rail travellers since the electric service to King's Cross was inaugurated in 1987. (*Photo Murray Brown*)

Revolution has come to the Cardiff Valley Line's passenger services. The passengers have come flocking back to the railways, aided by a sensible marketing strategy, provision of new services and new Sprinter trains. Two of these are featured here – one of the Cardiff Canton based Sprinters, No 150269, heads a Coryton–Taff Wells service at Radyr. The train is running on the new Cardiff City line – an old railway line but which has had a new almost circular service instigated offering Cardiff and district dwellers a vastly improved suburban service around the environs of the city. (*Photo Michael Rhodes*)

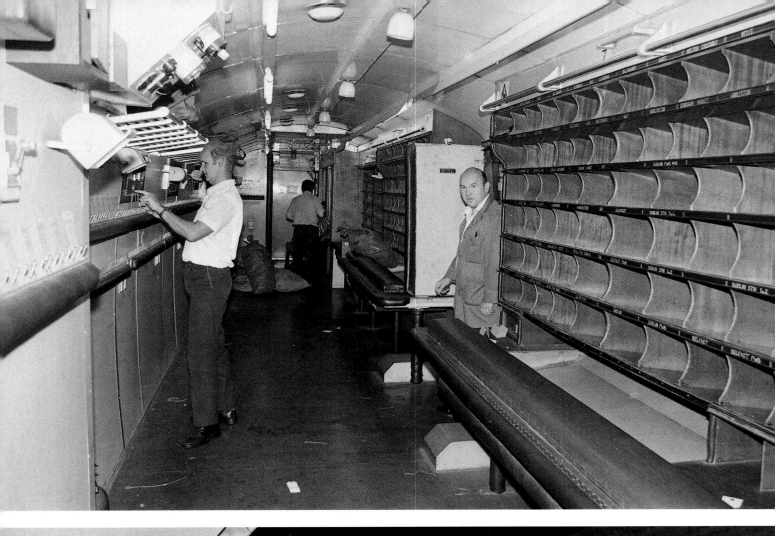

One of the most fascinating of all the duties seen on BR is the nocturnal postal sorting. These dedicated men travel the length and breadth of Britain in the Travelling Post Offices, sorting mail which is then transferred at major centres, particularly at Crewe and Derby for onward delivery. One of the Post Office trains which runs daily is the 20.00 Peterborough–Crewe. The staff were just getting ready for the night's work when seen at Peterborough. (*Photo Paul Savage*)

It is an education to travel on British Rail's only underground line – the Waterloo & City line which runs from Waterloo to Bank. The vehicles are of a smaller dimension than standard tube stock and serve thousands of commuters daily. The vehicles are brought to the surface by a lift at Waterloo when they require overhaul. This train is pictured at Waterloo. The railway is affectionately known as 'The Drain'. (*Photo Paul Savage*)

Down in the kitchen, something stirs! There's no finer pastime than dining on a train and it is fish today. Cook, Anthony Garbutt, prepares the fish dish in the kitchen of the return Executive service, the 11.41 Swansea–Paddington. (*Photo Deryck Lewis*)

On the day under the spotlight, the then Minister of Public Transport, David Mitchell, MP, was travelling home to his constituency in the West of England. Was he deliberating the fate of the Settle & Carlisle line when pictured in the 11.50 from Waterloo? He would not reveal any 'leaks' when asked! (*Photo Murray Brown*)

Why more of these splendid machines have not been introduced before now is one of life's mysteries, for the time saving is considerable. This was the scene on platform 3 at London's Victoria station as BR's coffers swelled by another huge amount. (*Photo Paul Savage*)

Alec Gray checks the air conditioning equipment on an HST power car No 43169 at St Philips Marsh depot, Bristol. Of interest is that the air conditioning equipment is virtually in use continuously, for as soon as the train enters the depot for maintenance or cleaning, a shore supply is plugged in to the front of the power car as can be seen in the picture to provide the power to energise the equipment. The equipment can then be tested. (*Photo Mike Goodfield*)

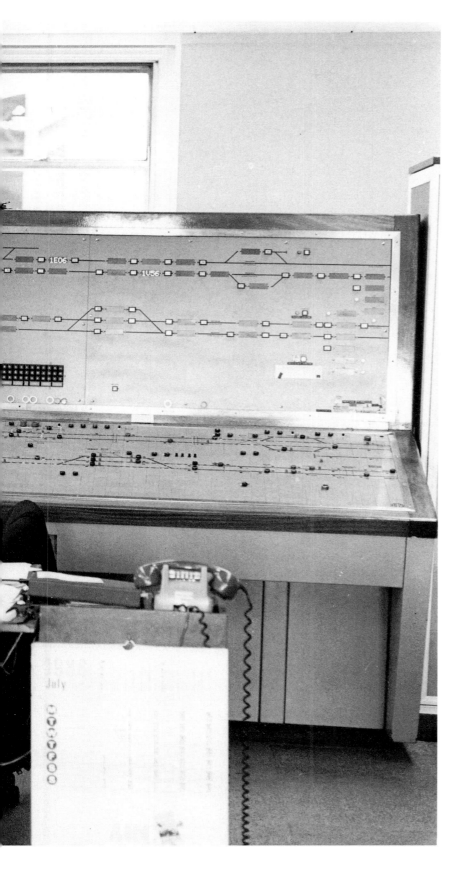

So that's why King's Cross concourse is so clean. Many of InterCity's terminals are now equipped with Terrazzo flooring which besides giving a far lighter and clean look, is, in fact, easier to keep clean. This unglamorous job was being undertaken at 08.15 when you might expect the place to be swarming with commuters. (*Photo Murray Brown*)

It is nearly twenty past six o'clock in Bristol signal power box and the signalman is at work controlling the lines which run from Filton Junction and Patchway to Hullavington to the east and Charfield to the north. This also includes Bristol Parkway station and Stoke Gifford freight yard. (*Photo Mike Goodfield*)

During the summer of 1988, the Venice Simplon Orient Express organisation operated a luxury land cruise in Wales using some of the VSOE Pullman cars. The itinerary included a run over the beautiful Central Wales line, not normally traversed by locomotive-hauled trains. The venture was not a success because of the drop in American tourists necessitating only a three coach train to cater for the numbers. Shrewsbury guard, Peter Hughes, waits to take the Pullman train out of Llandovery on the next stage of the tour. (*Photo Geoff Bannister*)

A fitter at Marylebone diesel depot checks the bolts on the brake gear of a class 115 multiple-unit vehicle. These units have been plying to and fro on the Chiltern Lines services for over twenty years but their days are now numbered. (*Photo Murray Brown*)

Remember the ferocious storms in October 1987? It was literally an ill wind which blew BR some good for there was a new traffic to be had – moving timber. This timber train was pictured at Fareham, headed by class 33 locomotive No 33006. Destinations for this timber traffic varied considerably, much of it being sent to the north of England. (*Photo Paul Savage*)

'May I recommend the fish, madam?' As passengers journey in air conditioned comfort on a an HST, staff are on hand with light refreshments or something more substantial. Chief Steward, Peter Murrin, presents the wine list to a passenger, while Stewardess, Paula Wilcox, waits to take her order. (*Photo Deryck Lewis*)

One of the many Speedlink trains run daily is the 16.10 Mossend, near Glasgow, to Gloucester which is electrically-hauled as far as Bescot. Heading southwards at Abingdon is this train in charge of class 85 No 85011. The consist comprises a variety of wagon types reflecting the differing commodities conveyed on the train. (*Photo Paul D. Shannon*)

(*Overleaf*) The same train pictured leaving Carlisle Kingmoor marshalling yard later the same day. (*Photo Paul D. Shannon*)

THE COMMUTER'S LOT IS NOW A HAPPY ONE!

The public has a love/hate relationship with railways and no more is this apparent than with the London commuter. One associates commuting with the capital, but throughout the country, millions of people use the train daily to their place of work.

The largest influx and exit of commuters takes place at London where BR's Network SouthEast provides most of the resources to cater for this colossal volume of traffic. Currently, the number of these vociferous travellers totals 458,000 – daily!

A brief moment to digest this figure will then be tempered with the realisation that BR has a major problem on its hands twice a day. The sheer logistics of providing trains to move this number of people is a creditable feat. To put it in perspective, a train arrives at a London terminal every eleven seconds during the morning peak.

BR has to work to government set standards, particularly financial. This affects BR in two ways regarding the commuter business. Not only is the government grant diminishing, thus forcing BR to provide more efficient services – no easy task, but the economics of providing trains in the morning and evening peaks does nothing for efficient use during the day. One of Network SouthEast's greatest successes has been the policy to attract off-peak business during the day to make better use of the stock. No less than 25% increase has been generated in this type of traffic.

The commuter has seen a dramatic change in many of his or her trains over the years. At the beginning of the 1980s (before the current business sectors of BR were formed) the commuter's train was often in the order of 20 years old. A massive programme of investment has been underway for successive years with the result that life for commuters has considerably improved with quieter, faster and more comfortable trains. There is now a vast chasm between the vintage diesel multiple-unit trains found on the Chiltern Lines out of Marylebone and the 100mph air conditioned 'Wessex Electrics' which ply between Weymouth and London Waterloo. These 24 units are the jewel in the crown for Network SouthEast. By 1992, two-thirds of all the stock used for commuting will be new.

The improvement in trains over the years has seen a steady expansion in the length of journeys undertaken by commuters. When the Southern Railway electrification started in 1933, people moved further away from London and this has continued ever since. Electrification reached Bournemouth in 1967 and whilst Bournemouth commuters were then subjects of discussion, nowadays they are an accepted way of life.

Long distance commuting has brought problems elsewhere to BR, for the boundaries of commuters are now well outside the Network SouthEast boundaries. The advent of the HST on the East Coast main line in March 1978 has brought a new dimension to commuter travellers – 125mph! A steady rise of these long distance travellers has seen many HSTs become overcrowded and BR, somewhat surprisingly to many gullible and naive members of the public, simply does not have empty £2m trains waiting to be brought into service when overcrowding takes place.

BR has been forced to protect its InterCity passengers by making life more difficult for commuters in two ways. First, BR has, in some instances, reduced the stops of HST in the peak period thus forcing commuters to catch the slower Network SouthEast trains. Second, the price per mile paid by long-distance commuters was far below that paid by Network SouthEast travellers and so fares paid by the former have risen dramatically.

There's more to commuting than just trains. The commuter wants more than this and he or she is getting it. There is a massive investment programme to improve all aspects of the rail traveller in London. These extend to major signalling schemes, such as those being undertaken at Liverpool Street and at Waterloo. Such multi-million pound works will have a beneficial effect on punctuality as the headways between trains will be improved, thus reducing the number of potential delays. Train punctuality is currently 92% overall. However, if you are a commuter on the Great Northern main line out of King's Cross, you are the most fortunate commuter of all, as punctuality is around 98%.

On the first floor of Euston House, the British Rail headquarters building at 24 Eversholt Street, Euston, London, can be found the *Rail News* office. Here the staff produce BR's own house journal which is issued free to all BR staff. Besides the staff based in London, the paper has two regional staff to assist in obtaining features and news, one based at Manchester and the other at Glasgow. (*Photo Murray Brown*)

The *Rail News* editor, Keith Horrocks, has held this position for over twenty years and there's nothing about editing that Keith does not know! He was preparing the August issue when caught at his desk on our review day. (*Photo Murray Brown*)

09.20 and it is already busy on the BR Press Desk. Chief Press Officer, Ian MacKellar (right) and his staff have to deal with hundreds of inquiries from the media. Diplomacy is a key word when working on this arduous duty, for the media men are always wanting a quote! (*Photo Murray Brown*)

The taking of this picture was no easy task, for the location was Blandford House at Marylebone station. Part of Blandford House is used to house BR's awesome computer system known as TOPS (Total Operations Processing System) which can handle hundreds of inquiries simultaneously. It is an on-line system which details the exact location of locomotives and rolling stock, state of payload, status of vehicle and maintenance data history, to name just a few. Security is therefore paramount and the picture shows some of the banks of computers which store and update all the data. The TOPS system is in operation around the clock throughout the year. (*Photo Murray Brown*)

Where it all happens! Euston House (24 Eversholt Street, Euston) is the headquarters building of the British Railways Board, in which Sir Robert Reid and his sector directors have their offices. Previously, this building was the headquarters of the London Midland Region before the regional HQ was moved to Birmingham. Following extensive renovation Euston House was occupied by BRB staff, many of whom vacated the previous HQ at 222, Marylebone Road, London. (*Photo Murray Brown*)

169

Cleanliness has improved in leaps and bounds, thanks to a concerted managerial drive aided by local staff initiatives such as 'Operation Sparkle'. Stations as well as trains are seeing the fruits of investment when it comes to cleaning.

Astonishingly, there are quoted instances of commuters actually complaining when their trains are refurbished with new decor and better lighting. Complaints have been received that trains are now so bright that commuters are unable to sleep!

BR's Network SouthEast business was launched in June, 1986, superseding the London & South East sector. It is managed with six sub-sectors which cover: Anglia (King's Cross and Liverpool Street), North (Euston), South East (Kent lines), South Central (Victoria to Brighton and associated lines), South West (Waterloo to Weymouth and Isle of Wight), Thames & Chiltern (Paddington and Marylebone routes). Expenditure is now running at just over £1,000m, with income at just over £800m and the government providing the support of £240m.

Curiously, with many commuters now using InterCity services to gain their place of work, it raises the question of politics in that why should one section of the travelling community (Network SouthEast) be government-supported in the form of subsidy whereas InterCity commuters are not subsidised? (InterCity as from April, 1988 receives no financial support from central government.)

So, as Mr Smith makes his daily trek from Brighton, one of nearly half a million fellow commuters, little does he realise that some 41,000 BR staff are involved in getting him and his colleagues to work and home again. As he reads his *Financial Times* with his 104 colleagues (this is the average train load) Mr Smith is a tiny cog in the busiest urban railway system in the world, serving a population of 18 million.

Fitter Martin Hallbrook replaces an axlebox cover from an HST power car at St Philips Marsh depot. Ultrasonic testing of axles is undertaken regularly to verify whether cracking is taking place. (*Photo Mike Goodfield*)

If it moves on BR, all locomotives, wagons and coaches have their own identification numbers and are marked with the vehicle's tare weight. Signwriter, Bob Croad, paints these details on a RRA type wagon No 110567 at Cardiff Cathays Carriage & Wagons Works, Cardiff. (*Photo Deryck Lewis*)

North London Line 2EPB No 6314 and sister No 6307 depart from Bognor Regis with empty coaching stock to West Worthing. The stock formed the 07.44 London Bridge–Bognor mail (*Photo Chris Wilson*)

Another view of HST maintenance shows Reg Northall checking the batteries of power car 43135 at St Philips Marsh depot. Most of HST maintenance is undertaken at night, but even so, some HST trains are only in the depot for a few hours before they are out earning revenue. (*Photo Mike Goodfield*)

Roy Taylor is the Shift Supervisor at St Philips Marsh depot where he is seen making an entry in the records. On the wall can be viewed the formations of the HSTs. Vehicles are swapped if required for maintenance purposes and the changes are duly logged so as to provide an easy visual guide to every train set formation. (*Photo Mike Goodfield*)

The Research Department's locomotives and rolling stock have their own distinctive livery and brighten the railway scene. One of its locomotives is a class 31 No 97204, which is seen on the Mickleover test track. Besides working on the two test tracks, Research Department traction also works over the British Rail system. (*Photo John Tuffs*)

Stewardess, Jackie Connors and
trainee Stewardess, Donna Williams,
serve a passenger on the 11.41 return
Executive service from Swansea to
Paddington. Catering on InterCity
trains is operated by InterCity's On-
Board Services arm, whilst station
catering is managed, in the main, by
Travellers Fare, although there are
still some privately operated buffet
facilities such as those found at
Malton, Huddersfield and
Stalybridge. (*Photo Deryck Lewis*)

Although Hereford is a long way
from the Network SouthEast
boundary some services to this
pleasant city use NSE stock. This
was the case with the illustrated
example showing a Hereford bound
service at Honeybourne behind class
50 loco No 50015 *Valiant*. (*Photo
Steve Turner*)

177

There are thousands of railway enthusiasts in Great Britain and they can be seen at the larger stations enjoying their hobby and taking photographs (95% of enthusiasts own a camera). It is a much maligned hobby, particularly by the media who portray enthusiasts as mentally sub-normal. Even BR, surprisingly, does not encourage railway enthusiasm despite its obvious financial benefits (captive market). Here, 14-year-old Gareth Morgan of Burnley is seen at Cardiff Central photographing one of Cardiff Canton depot's new class 150/2 Sprinter units, set No 150262. (*Photo Deryck Lewis*)

Double headed class 47s are not common but this scene occurs twice a day. The 06.14 Stanlow–Leeds and the 06.56 Stanlow–Jarrow tanks are normally double-headed as far as Miles Platting, sometimes to Castleton, and on rare occasions even as far as Healey Mills. Two class 47s storm through Manchester Victoria towards Miles Platting bank. (*Photo Steve Chapman*)

The atmosphere of privatisation hangs over the shed at Aberystwyth as well as the exhaust of the locomotive – No 7 *Owain Glyndwr*. BR's last three steam locomotives, Nos 7, 8 and 9 are part of the Vale of Rheidol narrow gauge line which runs from Aberystwyth to Devil's Bridge. VOR chief fitter, Chris Newton, standing by the water column, supervises the preparation of this powerful tank locomotive. (*Photo Andrew Bannister*)

With only hours to go before
withdrawal, class 45 No 45128
sweeps across Crewe North Junction
with the 1D79 1740 Liverpool Lime
Street–Dover Priory parcels service.
(*Photo Eddie Bellass*)

SIGNALS, POINTS AND BARRIERS – ALL IN A DAY'S WORK

A day in the life of a signal technician is, in reality, a look at what takes place during an eight hour shift. Many railwaymen throughout the country work to a three-shift system – vital if the railway is to operate around the clock. The technician under the spotlight here is based at Peterborough and is one of a team of trouble-shooters who attend all manner of signalling equipment, not just to rectify faults, but also to give maintenance. He is supported by a technical officer and a senior technician.

All signalling faults, when they occur, are passed on by the signalman to Fault Control which works in conjunction with operating staff in the regional control office. They assess the situation and, if there is more than one fault in that area, the technicians are sent to the fault with top priority, that is to say, the one which is delaying trains.

The time is 06.10 and a No 2 AWS (automatic warning system) fault is reported at Huntingdon by the driver of the 05.43 Peterborough–King's Cross train. An AWS is a magnet, situated in the middle of the track, which gives the driver a visible and audible warning of what aspect the signal, which the train is approaching, is showing. For a green signal, a bell rings and for a single yellow or double yellow and a red signal, a horn sounds. When the horn sounds, the driver must cancel it out, otherwise the brakes are applied automatically. The No 2 AWS fault is when the driver hears a horn instead of receiving a bell at a green signal. Various other types of AWS faults are also given numbers.

At 06.16 the team is on its way, miles to go, and most of it on the notorious A1 road. Depending on the traffic, it could take 45 minutes to get there.

06.50 and the three-man team is on site. The technician has his lookout equipment ready, whilst his colleagues have the meter and tools. A strength and polarity meter is used on AWS faults. This gives the technicians an indication as to the reliability of the magnet.

On arrival at the magnet, it is evident that the cable to it has been cut on the adjacent line, probably by the previous night's track tamping machine. The cable is repaired, and then a test is carried out on the AWS, using the strength and polarity meter, to ensure that the fault has been rectified and that the indication corresponds with the signal. The signal is then booked with the signalman in the power box and with Fault Control.

Back at the depot at 08.20, it is time for a cup of tea and some breakfast.

An hour passes, and suddenly the phone rings. A ground-position light (sub) signal in the carriage sidings has a red light out.

On the way there, the bleeper sounds with the message that a track circuit shows occupied at Little Bytham on the up fast-line. Trains are being diverted onto the up slow-line. On main lines, sections of track are electrically isolated and a small current passed through. When a train reaches the section of track, its wheels short circuit the current which in turn activates a relay (switch) and puts the signal behind the train to red.

With a change of direction, the technician and his colleagues leave the sub-signal (because it is considered low priority) and head north.

Forty minutes later, having arrived at the location, it is found that there is low voltage on the track, with only 1.5 volts instead of the normal 6 volts. This indicates that there is a short circuit; something is touching both rails, causing the track circuit to show occupied when in reality it should not. When a track circuit shows occupied, the signal at the rear automatically shows a red signal.

On walking along the section of track controlled by the track circuit, it is noticed that an electrification traction-return-bond (used for earthing metal structures) is touching both the positive and negative rail, causing the short circuit. With this moved away, the fault clears, and all is duly tested and declared in order. Then, it's back to the van and back to the signal in the sidings.

It is now 11.30 and the blown 110-volt bulb in the sub-signal is replaced. Fortunately, no trains have been delayed.

Returning to the depot, the bleeper sounds again. This time a set of points at Werrington Junction requires attention. The signalmen has not got detection in the reverse position. (This is not personal! It means that

A familiar sight in North London are the class 308 Electric Multiple Units which date from 1961. Their days are clearly numbred with the introduction of the new class 321 units. Here 308994 is seen passing Woodgrange Park heading for the Great Eastern's terminus at Liverpool Street. (*Photo Alex Dasi-Sutton*)

A pool of class 56 locomotives are used to haul the Leicestershire aggregate trains, most of which head for the home counties. No 56063 *Bardon Hill* is pictured near Desborough Summit near Kettering, with a stone train from Loughborough to Haywards Heath. (*Photo Mick Alderman*)

One of the familiar freight trains which runs frequently along the North Wales coast line conveys sulphur to Amlwch on Anglesey where Associated Octel use it in the manufacture of petrol additive.

Vintage HKV wagons are still used for this service and this picture shows the train, which starts at Mostyn Dock en route to Amlwch at Abergele. Powering the train is class 31 No 32312. (*Photo Larry Goddard*)

the signalman is not receiving confirmation that the point blades have actually travelled their full length and are hard up against the check rail. Only when detection is confirmed can the signal be cleared and a train allowed through.) The fault has stopped a Spalding–Peterborough train from coming off the branch onto the up slow-line.

After a 20-minute drive through the heavy traffic, the nearest access point is gained. This time a point-machine crank-handle is included amongst the tools, in case the handle has to be inserted into the point machine and the blades of the points moved manually across.

The problem is soon discovered. A ballast train has passed over the points whilst they were in the normal (straight) position, and some ballast has dropped into the slide chairs of the open points. This has prevented the blades, known as a 'switch', from fitting up to the rail sufficiently

There are many freight trains which run on the Southern Region, particularly aggregate trains. These have increased since the Channel Tunnel construction began. Cliffe, in Kent, despatches numerous aggregate trains and this picture shows a returning empty train from Purley. It is passing Redhill, hauled by two of the Southern Region's class 33 locomotives, Nos 33211 and 33057. (*Photo Alex Dasi-Sutton*)

close for the signalman to obtain detection. With the offending stones removed, the points are tested and the train is allowed to proceed on its way after a 35-minute delay.

Back to the depot and a bite of lunch. Not for long! At 12.45, Fault Control rings again and advises that the auto-half barriers at Peakirk have failed in the down position. All auto-half barrier crossings are designed to fail with the barriers against the traffic as a safeguard.

The local police are present, as is a handsignalman, and the barriers have been put under local control. This is where the handsignalman can operate the barriers on the command of the signalman in the signalbox. The police are in attendance to ensure that no motorists try to go around the lowered barriers. The first job is to check with the signalman that no trains are in the vicinity. In the metal cabinets adjacent to the barriers

are housed various electrical relays (switches) and these are checked to verify if all are in order. It is immediately noticed that one of the treadle relay contacts is in the down position instead of being up.

Treadles are one of the means by which a train automatically sets off the barrier lowering sequence. They are boxes which contain contacts, and the whole assembly is clamped to the side of a rail. Contacts are connected to an arm which, in turn, is pressed down by the flange of a wheel. Therefore, as the train wheel hits the treadle arm, the contacts are opened and the barriers start to lower.

Why are the contacts in the down position? The problem is that there is no voltage on one of the wires. Why? A walk to the next location box (a metal cabinet with electrical equipment) provides the answer. On close inspection, a cable is found which has had its insulation chewed by mice, thus causing the electrical fault. Vermin attacks on cables are a fairly frequent occurrence in the world of railway signalling, but fortunately it is a fairly simple job to mend damaged cable, and the fault is remedied straightaway.

Driving back to the depot in the yellow van it is nearly 14.00 and time to go home. The next shift will take over, and continue to offer a speedy back-up service for any reported signalling fault, which can include points and barrier crossings as well as actual signals. The technician's important job is one which rarely receives any publicity, and yet it is vital to the smooth day-to-day running of the railway system.

The 6F16 14.30 Llandudno Junction-Warrington Walton Old Junction, Speedlink service commences its journey behind class 47 No 47291 *Port of Felixstowe*, conveying a variety of wagon types. (*Photo Larry Goddard*)

Two of Cardiff's class 37 locomotives, 37141 and 37207 return the 1200 empty tanks from Langley to Robertston. The locomotives used on this and similar petroleum duties are the most extensively worked in the country, some being utilised up to 18 hours a day. (*Photo John C Baker*)

Nobody ever knows what a signal technician looks like, for all you usually see is the rear view! This one was caught at work on the East Coast main line where he was checking electrical circuits. He is inspecting the wiring in the metal cabinet known as a location box. These house relays (switches) which govern the operation of track circuits, signals and automatic half barriers. (*Photo Murray Brown*)

Tom Costello has an important job. He is one of five security men who supervise the smooth running of the BRB headquarters building at Euston House. Every person entering has to secure Tom's approval before being allowed to enter. 'Excuse me, sir, where is your pass?' (*Photo Murray Brown*)

The branch line from Stourbridge Junction to Stourbridge Town in the West Midlands is the shortest line in the country at ¾ mile long. Single car class 122 unit No 55033, the only one in Midline livery, is seen on the line arriving at the Junction station. (*Photo Stephen Widdowson*)

ACKNOWLEDGEMENTS

The photographs are acknowledged to their takers at the end of the captions. Unless otherwise stated the text is by Murray Brown. Other contributors are David St John Thomas ('A Day in the Life of British Rail' and 'One Traveller's Day'), Geoffrey Kichenside ('Newton Abbot Snapshot') and Paul Shannon ('The Railfreight Scene').

Thanks are given to British Rail and its many staff (and some passengers!) who helped make this book possible.

INDEX

Page numbers in *italic* indicate illustrations